Just a few photos from Carlisle,Windermere, Morecambe, Edinburgh and Glasgow

----

-This is just some photos, simply because nature/scenery/city photos are nice to look at. You might not be able to go there,because it's expensive for you to go there, because you are ill or any other reason. But you can look at photos.

Sometimes I paint or draw the photos-not of people though.

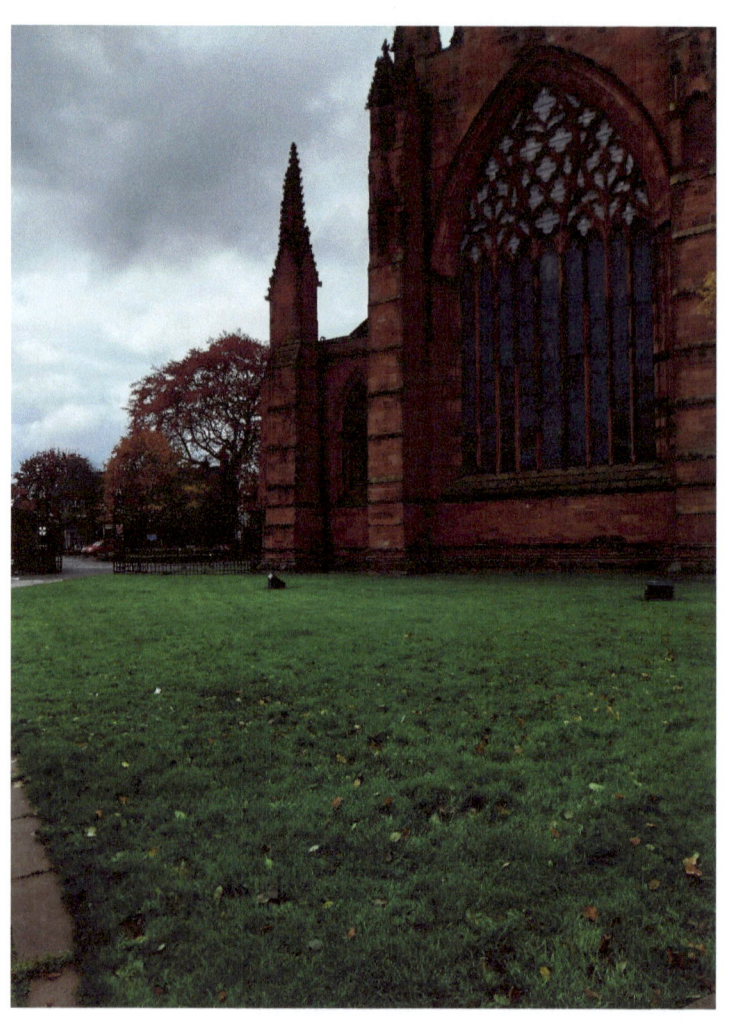

Carlisle Cathedral

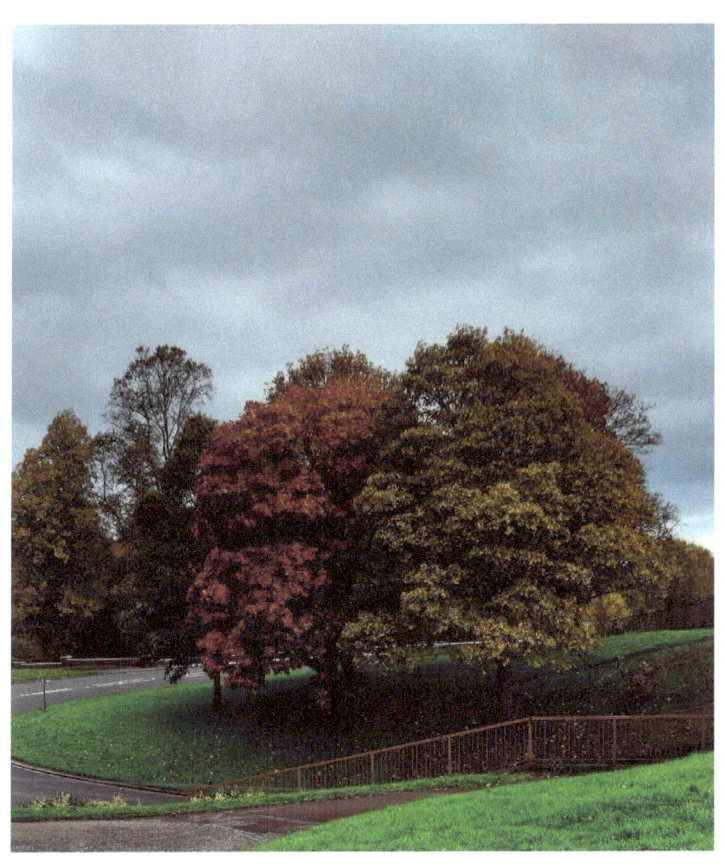

Carlisle,Cumbria

Bitts park

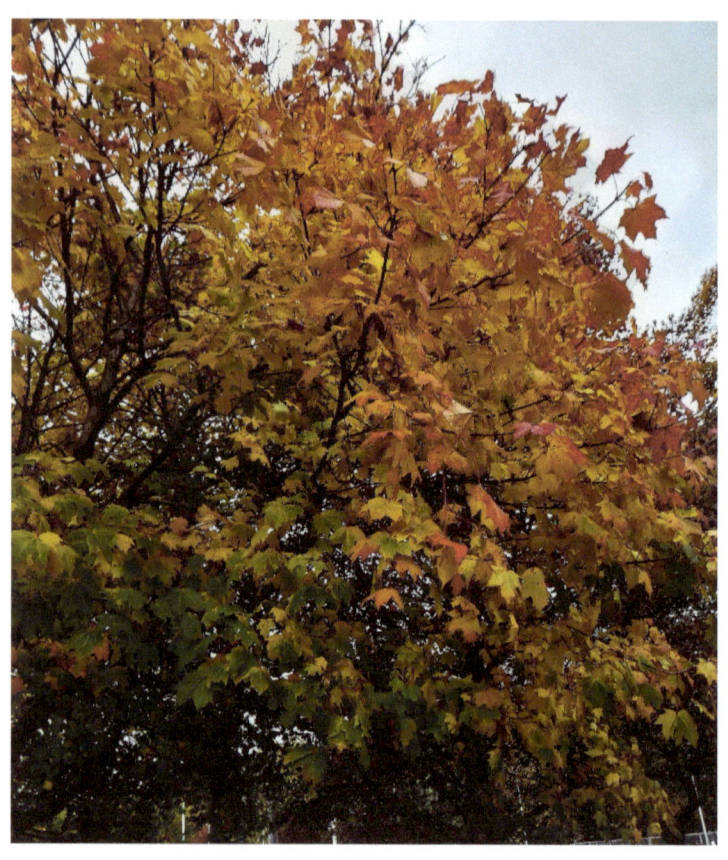

Autumn tree

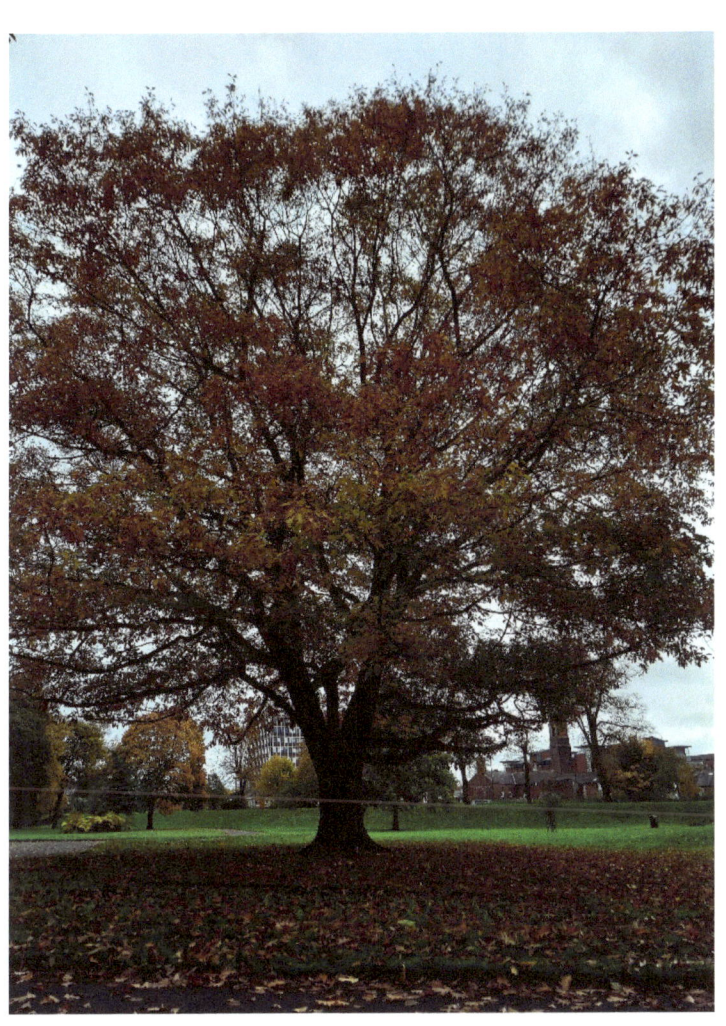

Autumn trees in the park

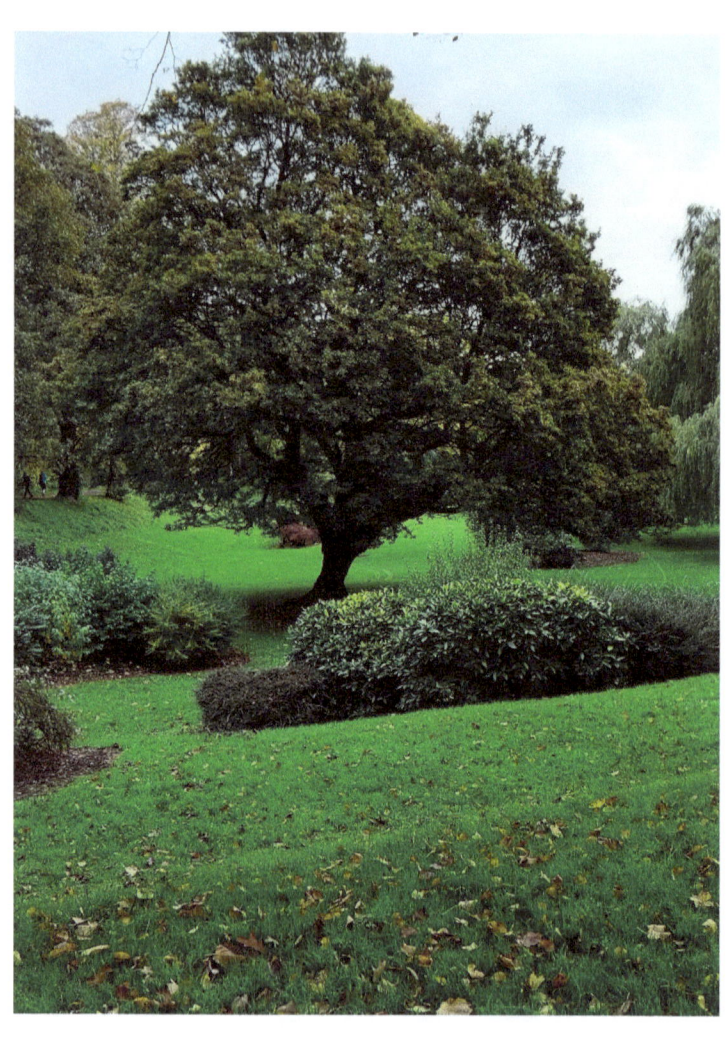

Trees and bushes in the park

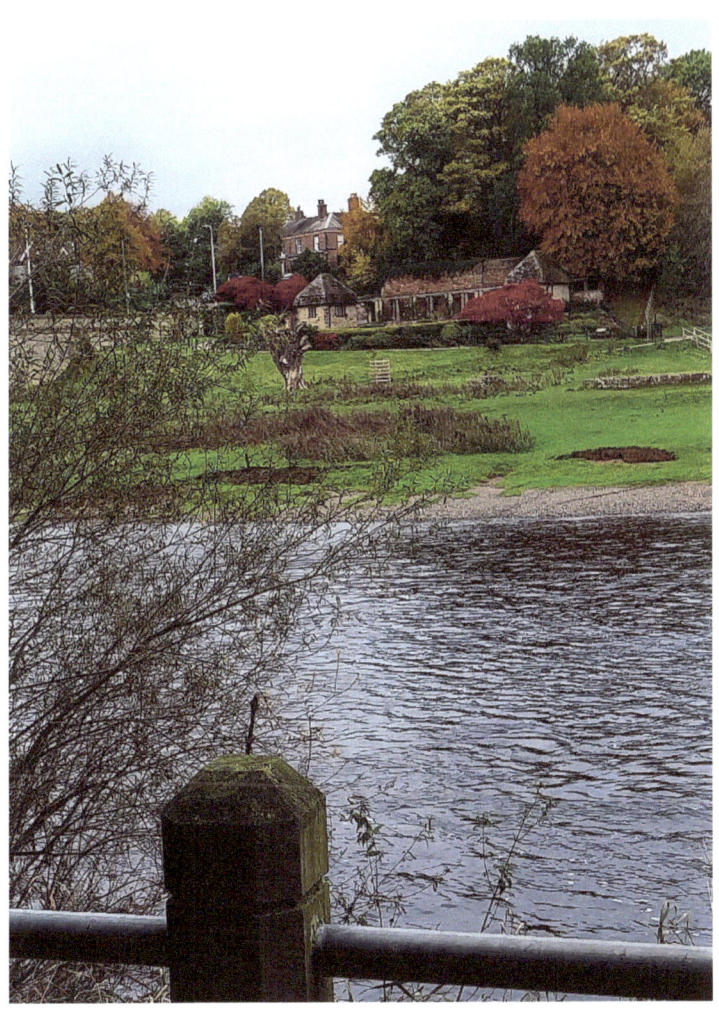

Autumn ,colours,houses,river Eden

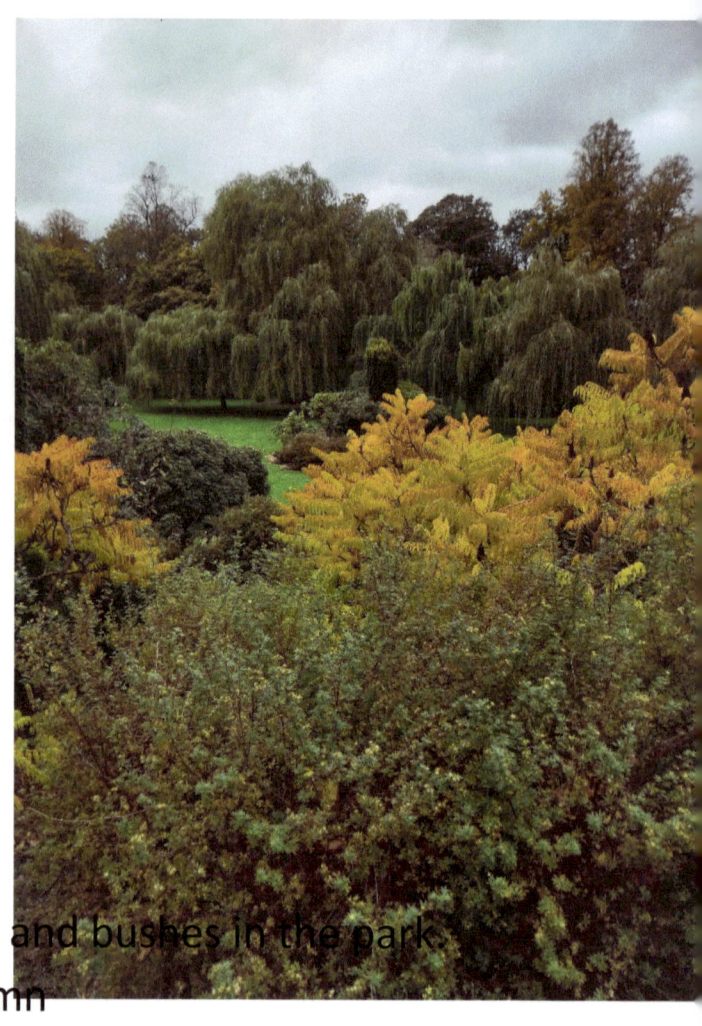

Trees and bushes in the park.
Autumn

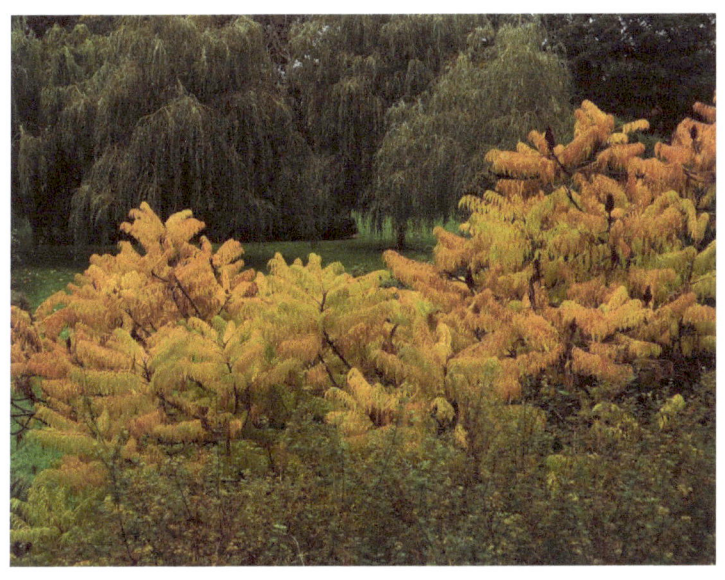

Trees in the park,autumn

I think it's beautiful and also nice to paint or draw

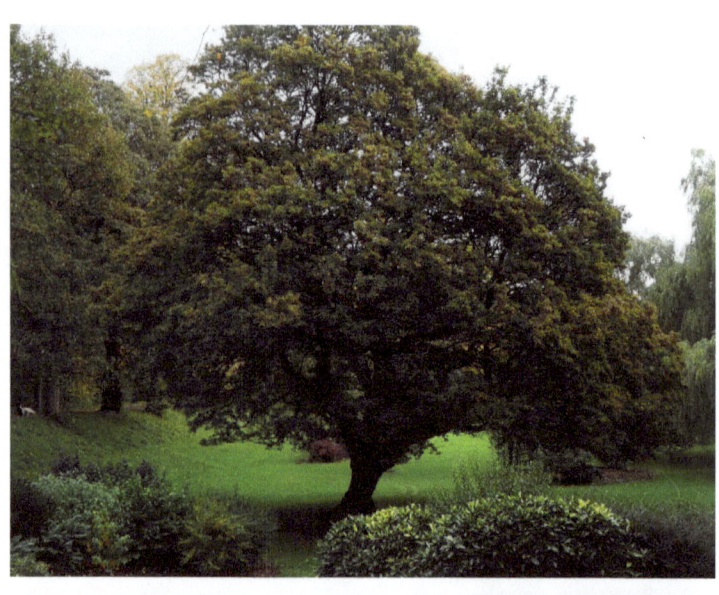

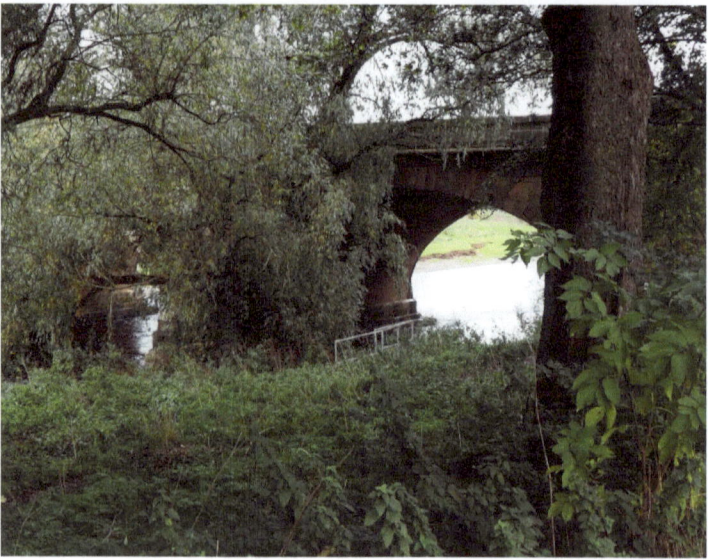

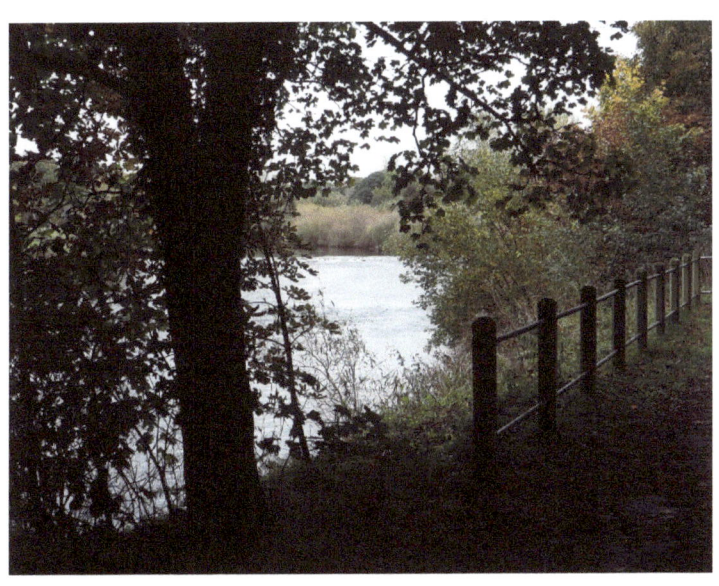

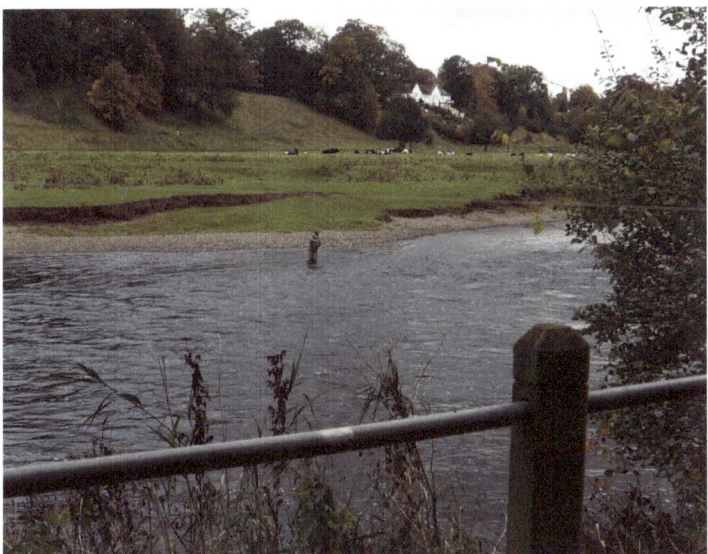

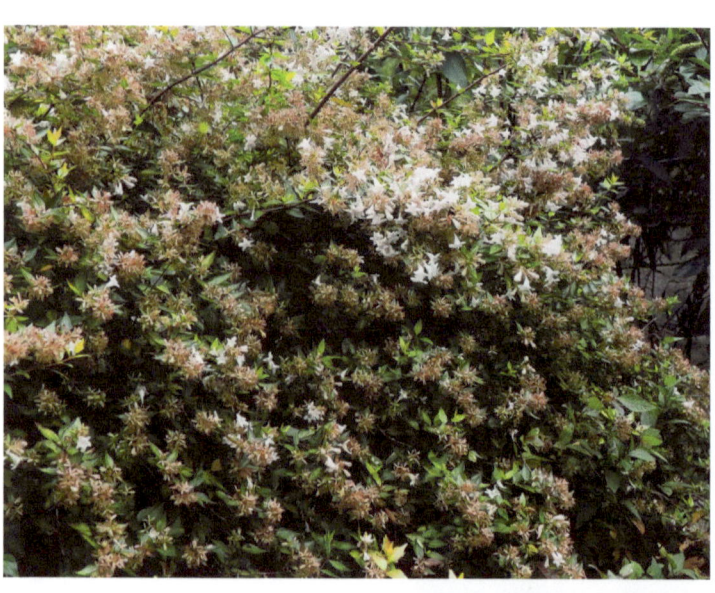

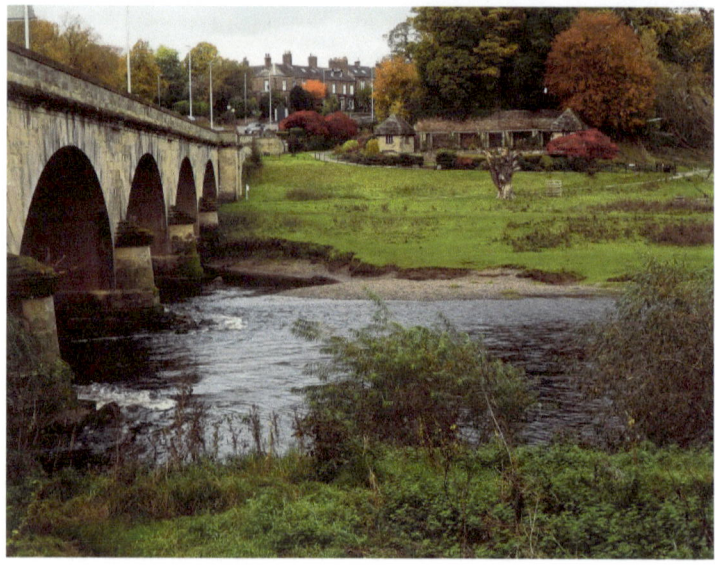

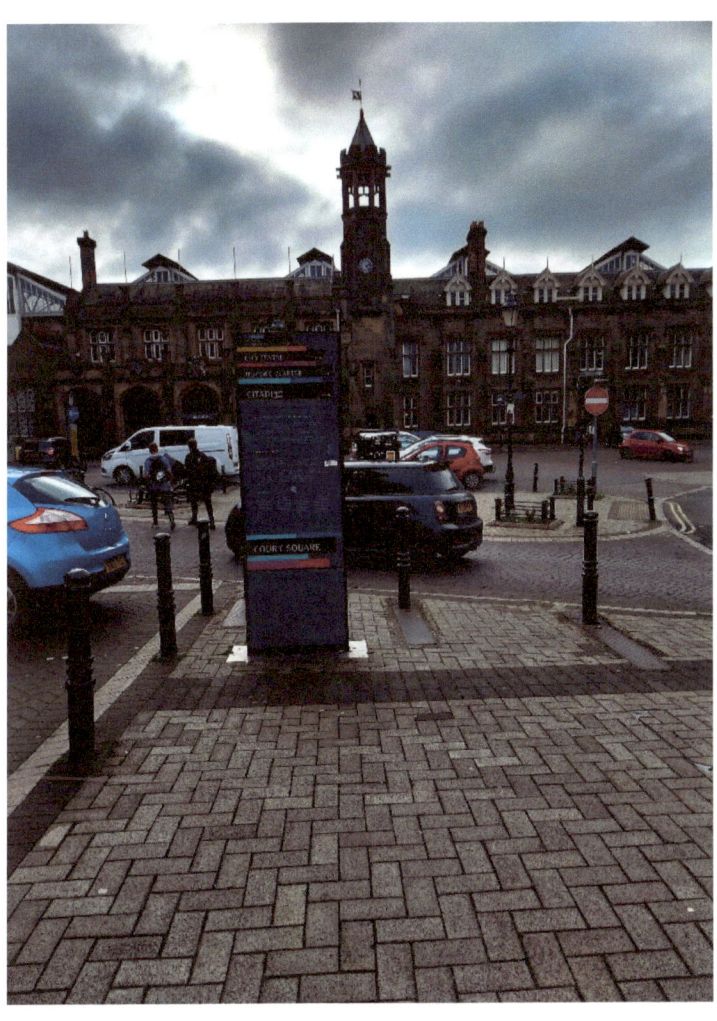

Carlisle trainstation

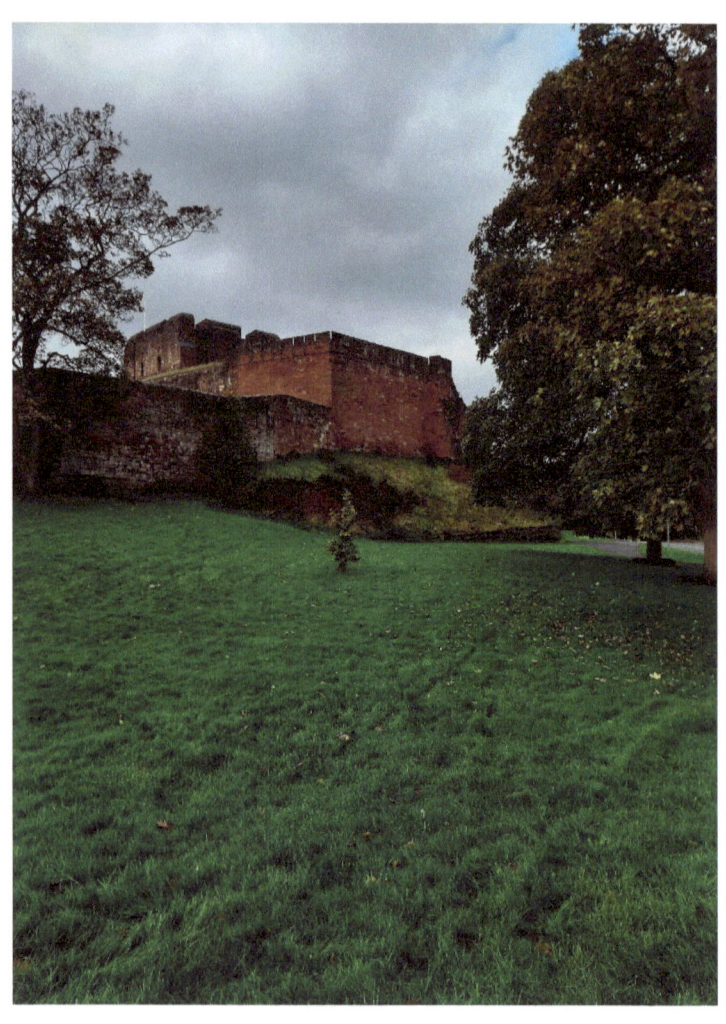

Carlisle castle from the side

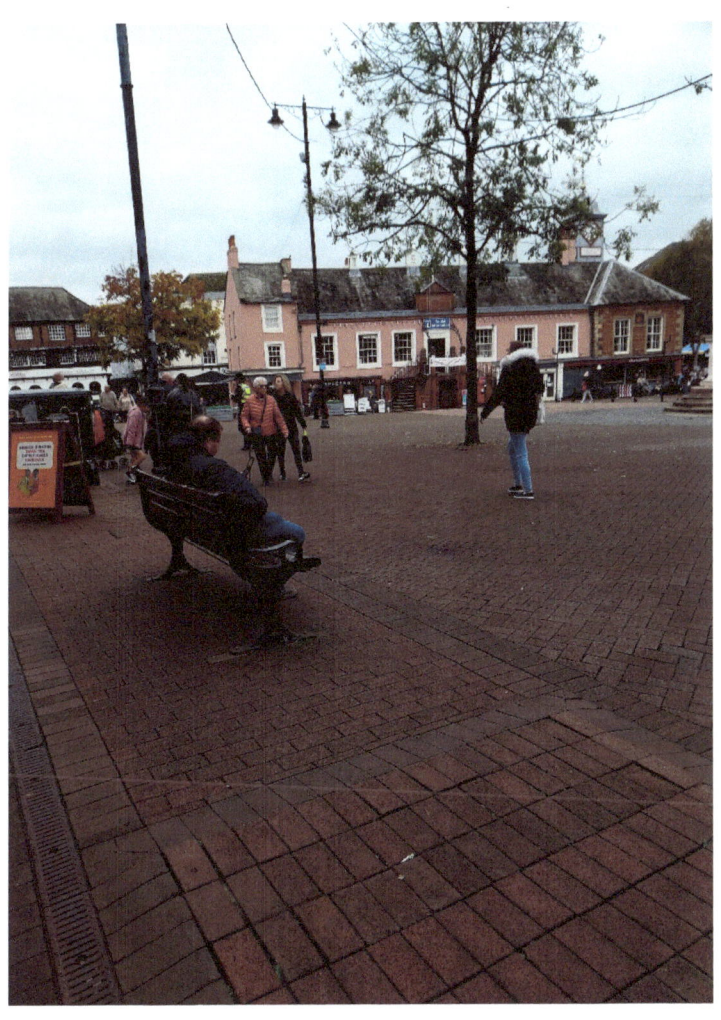

Carlisle city centre,in front of tourist information building,afternoon

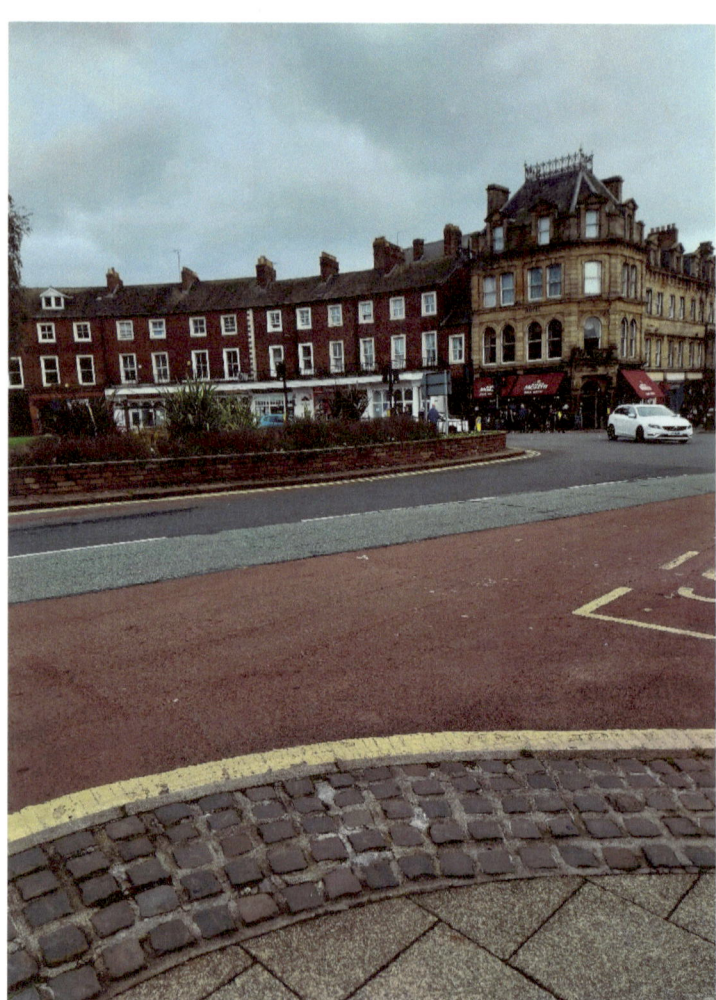

Windermere

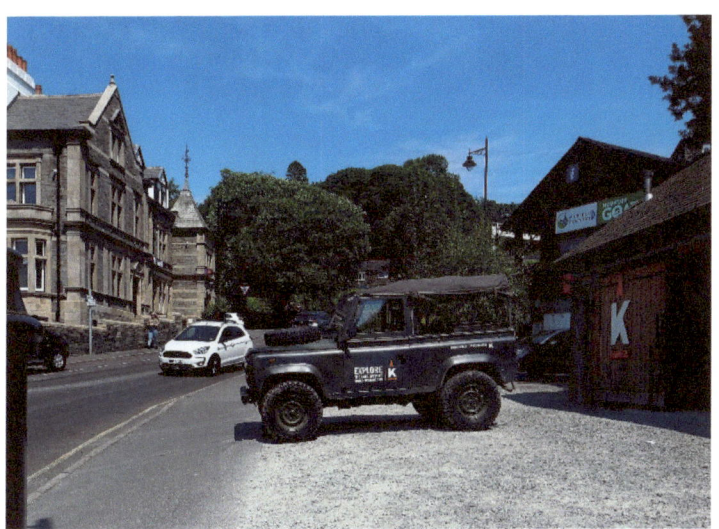

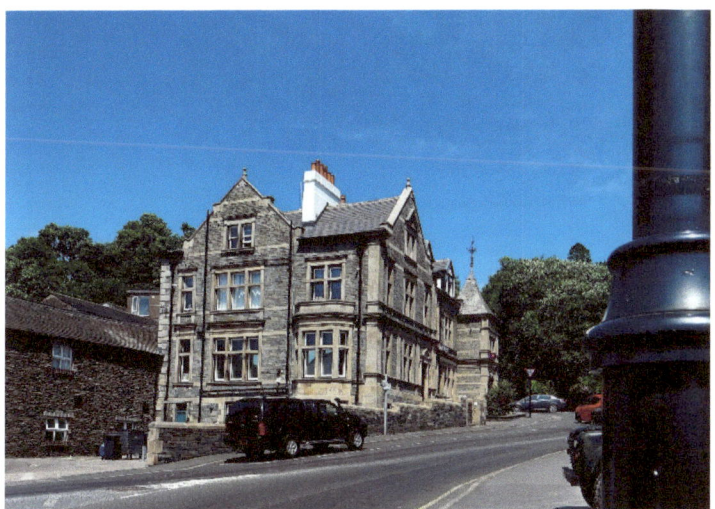

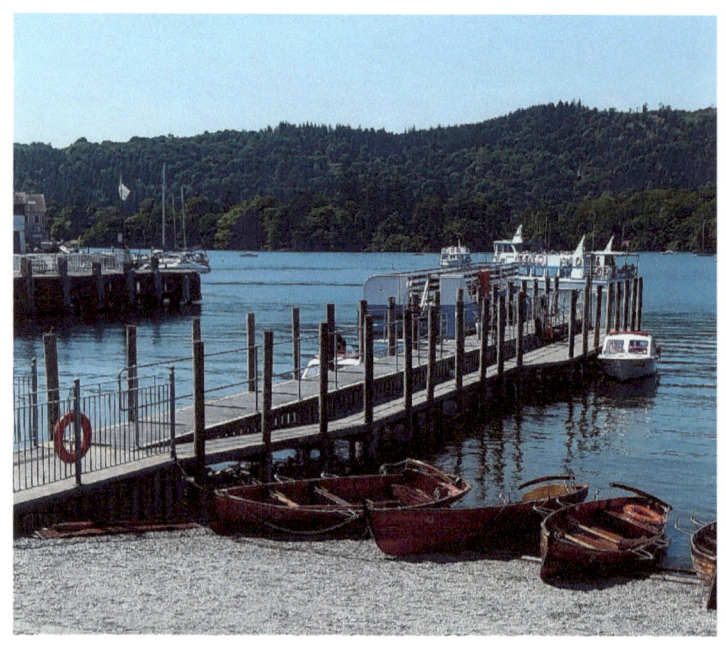

Windermere and lake
windermere,boats

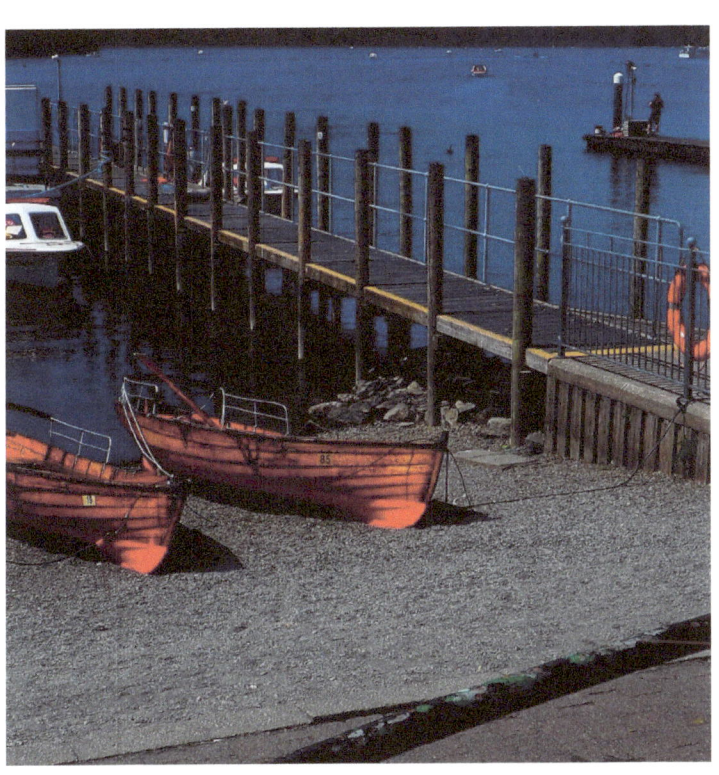

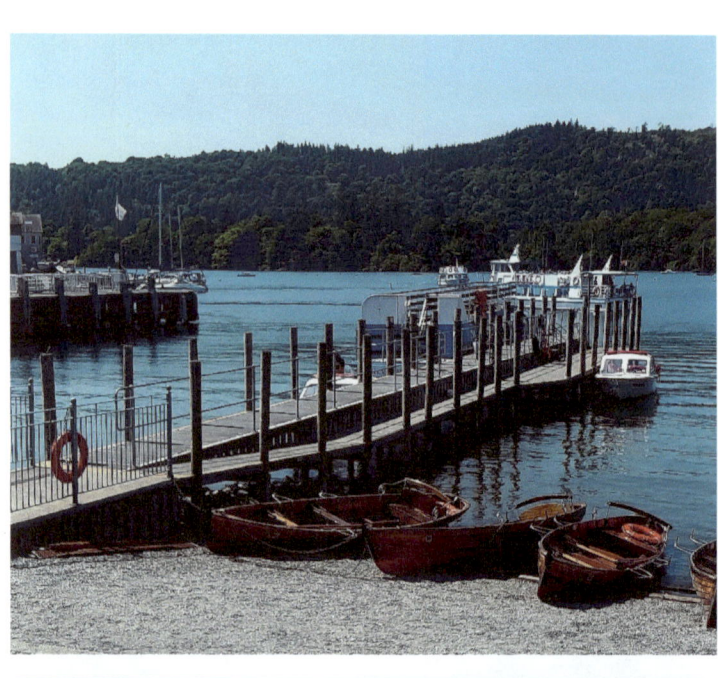

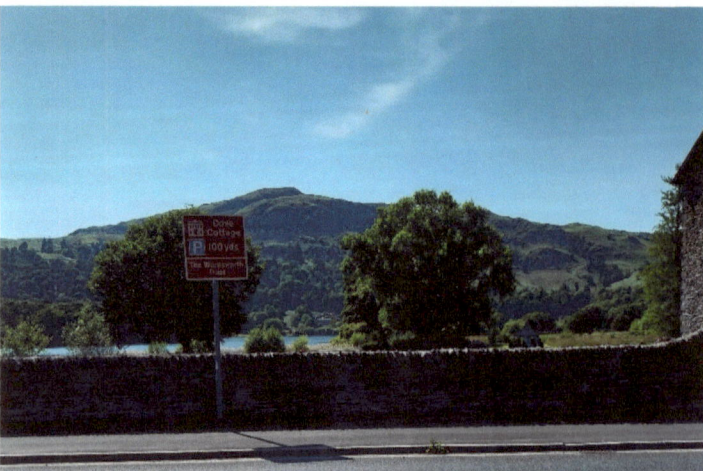

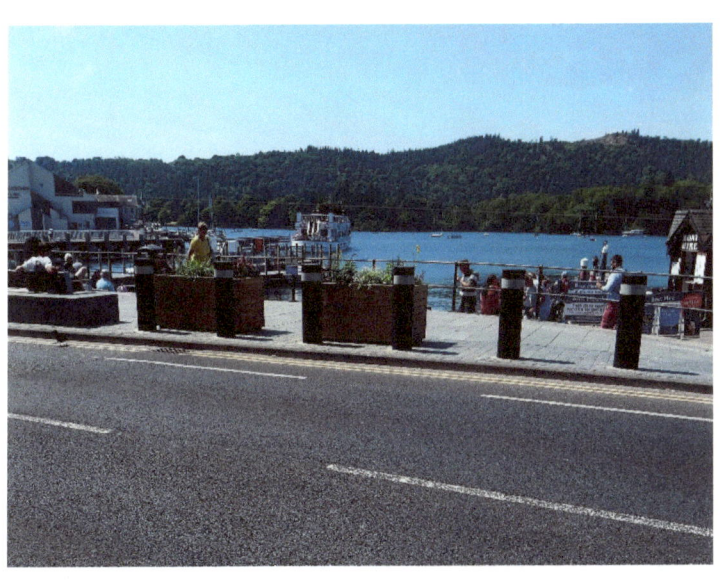

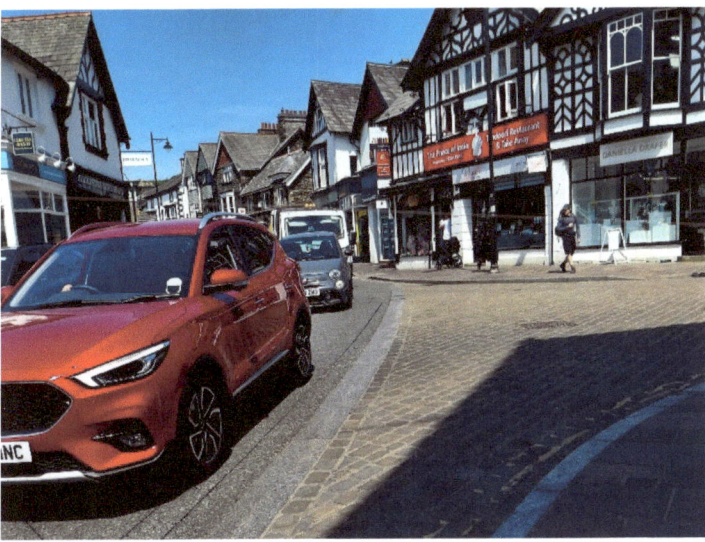

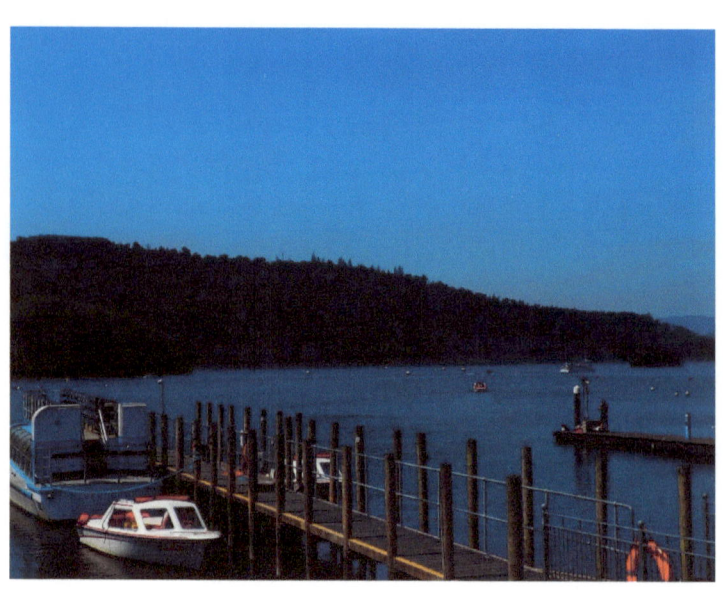

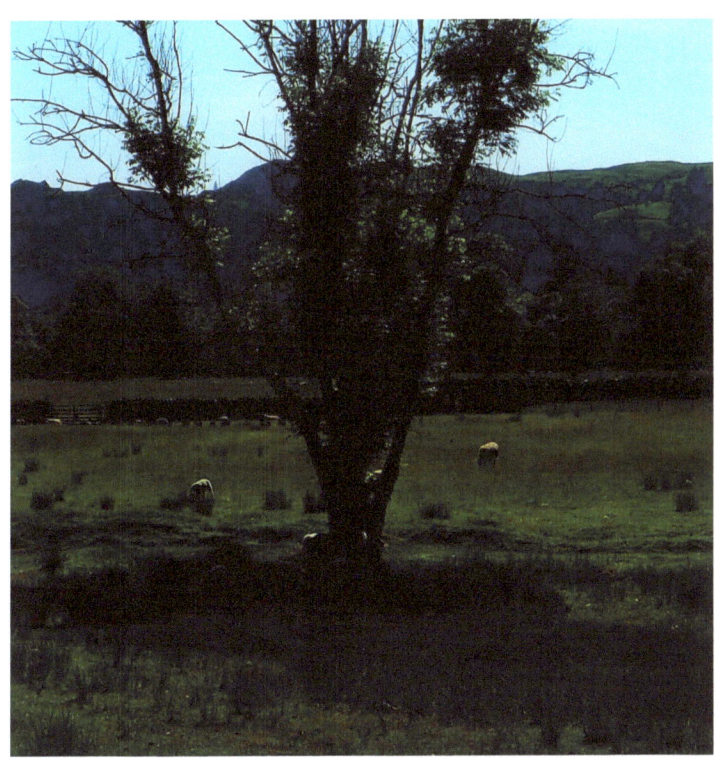

Tree,mountains ,sheep..

Morecambe

Morecambe wintergardens

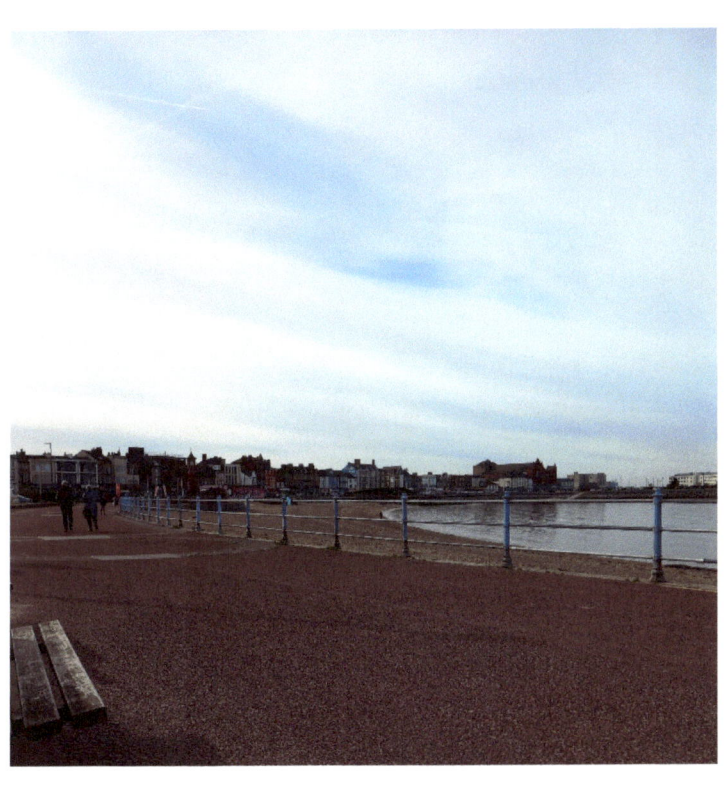

Morecambe
central,clocktower,houses

Morecambe bay,water

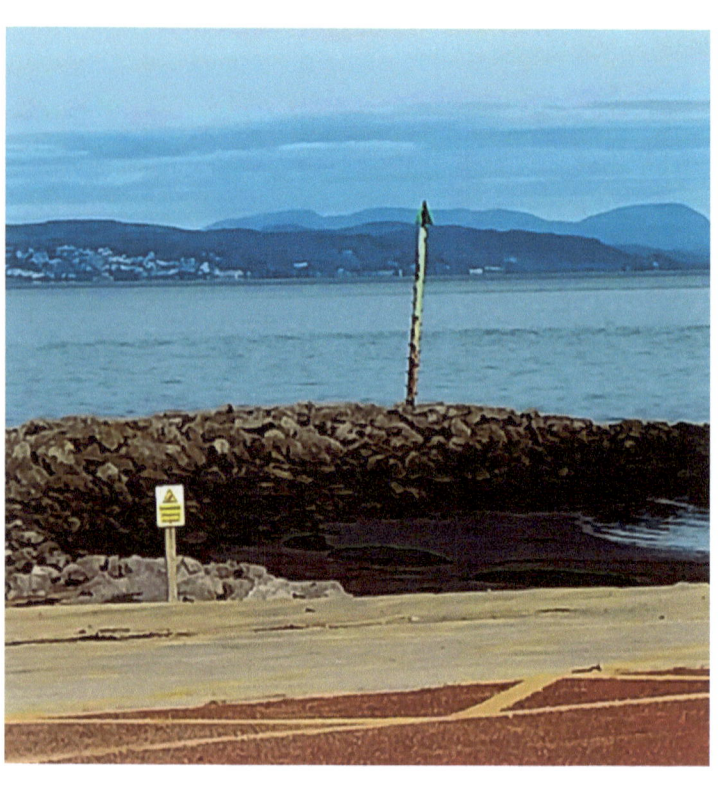

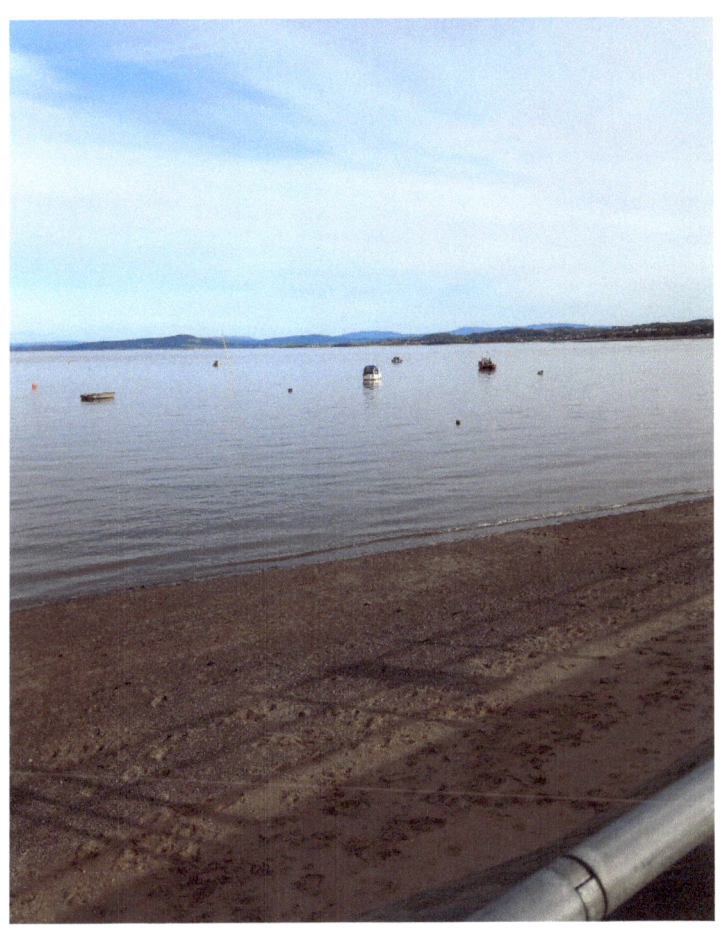

Morecambe bay at Bare

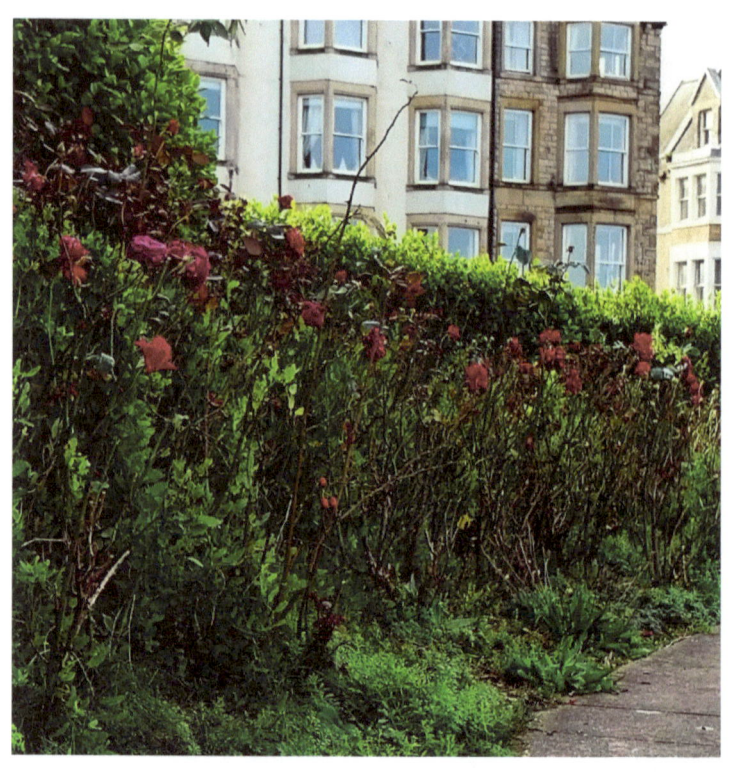

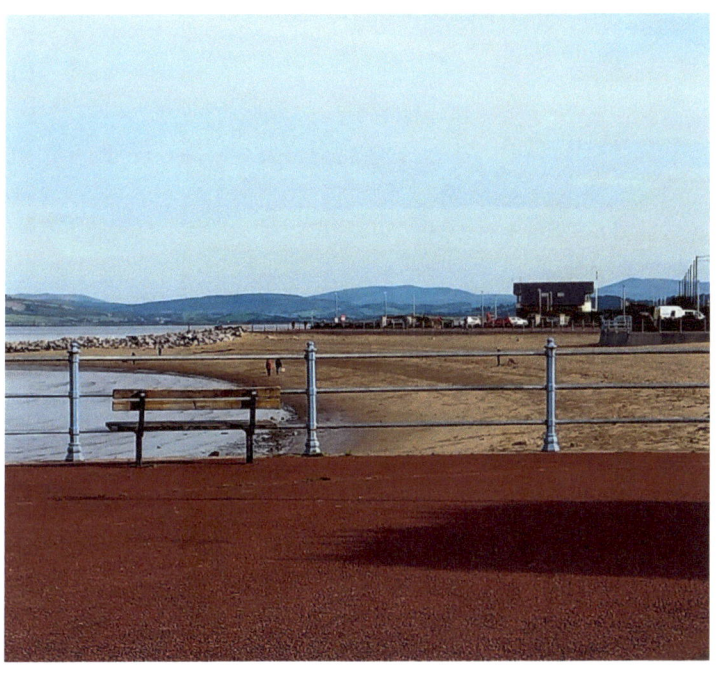

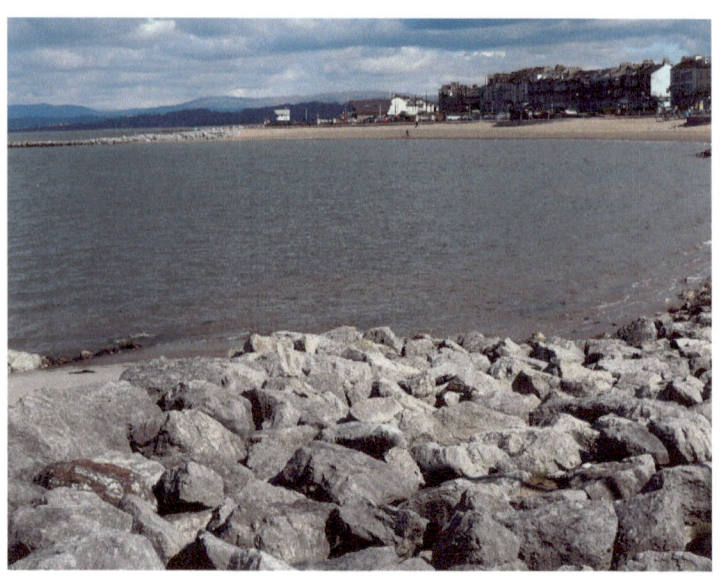

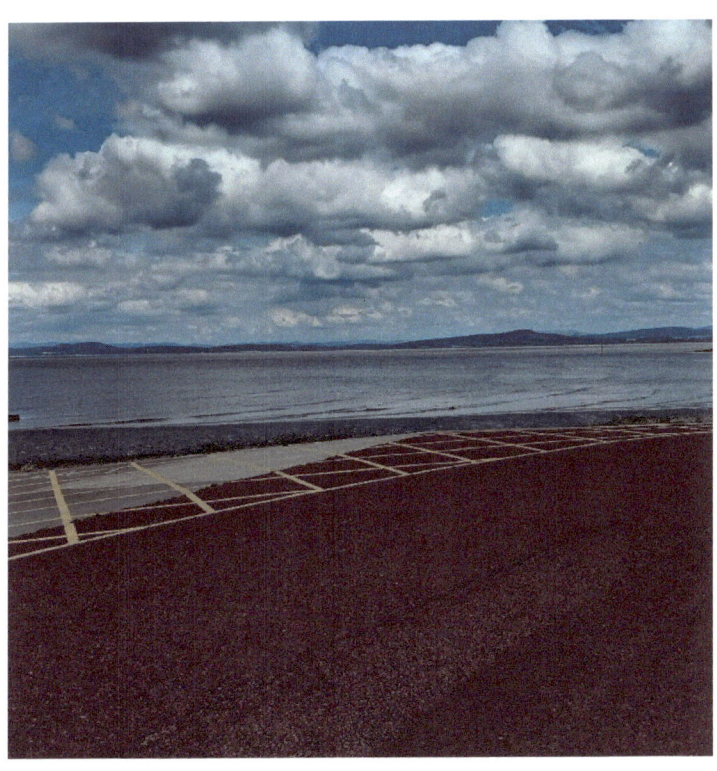

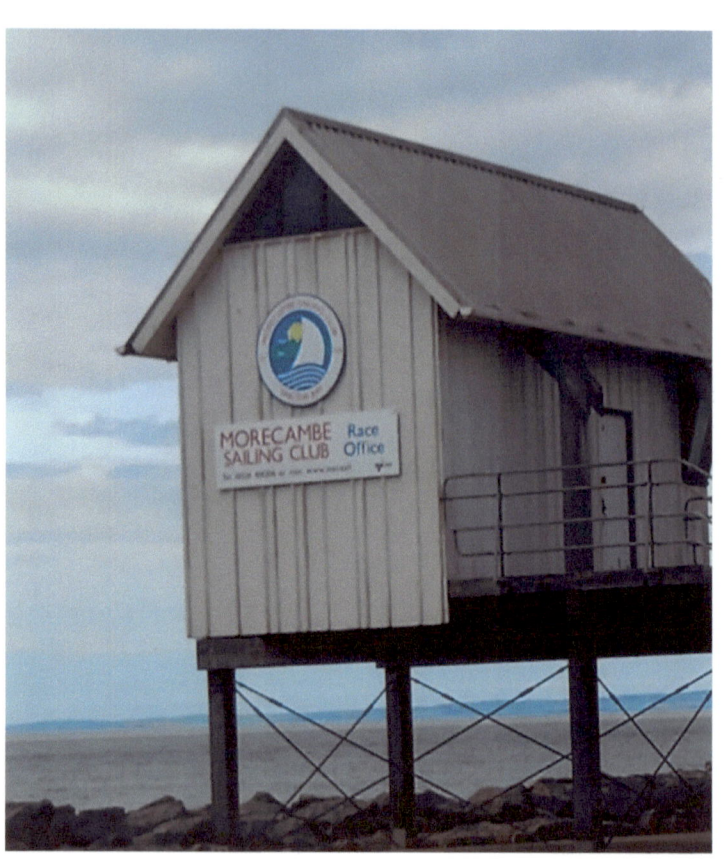

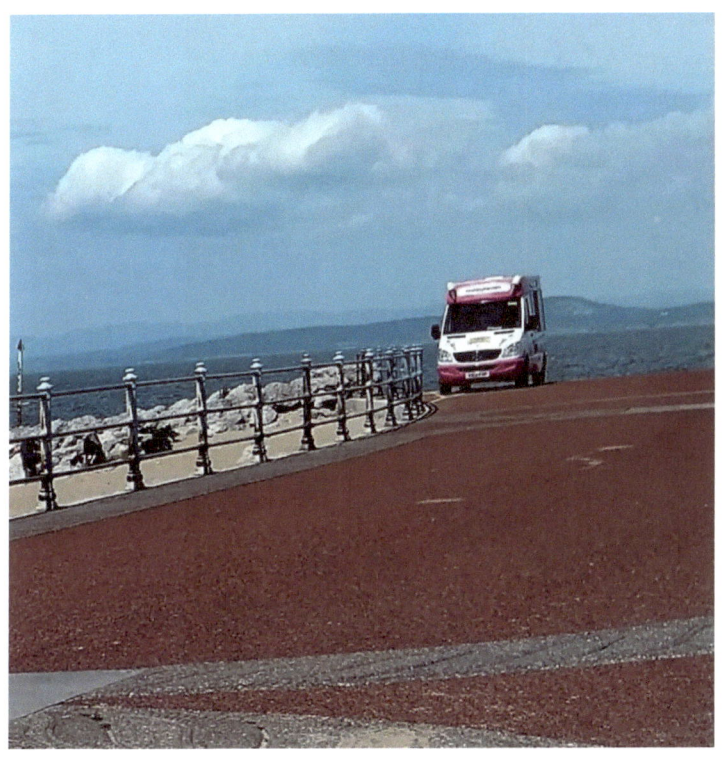

Ice-cream van

Edinburgh

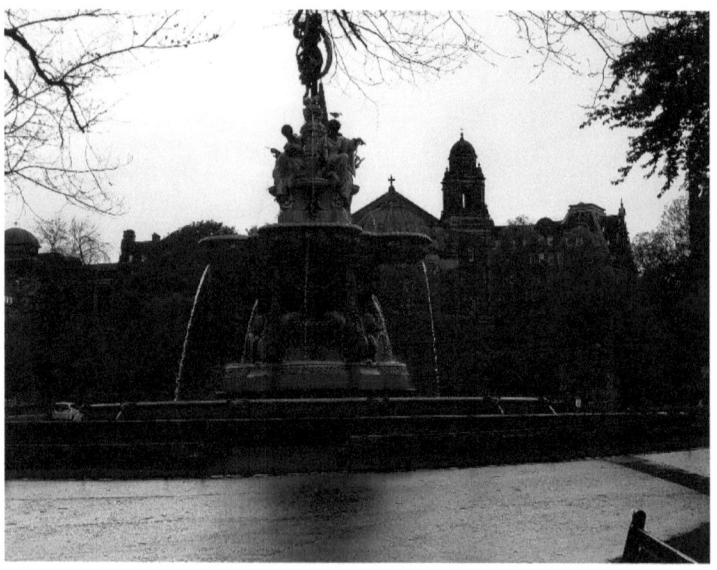

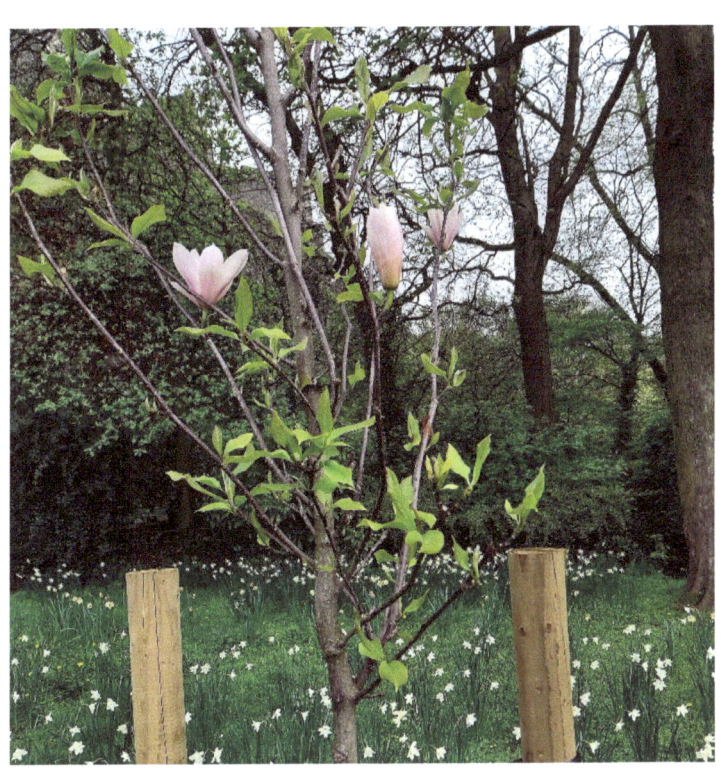

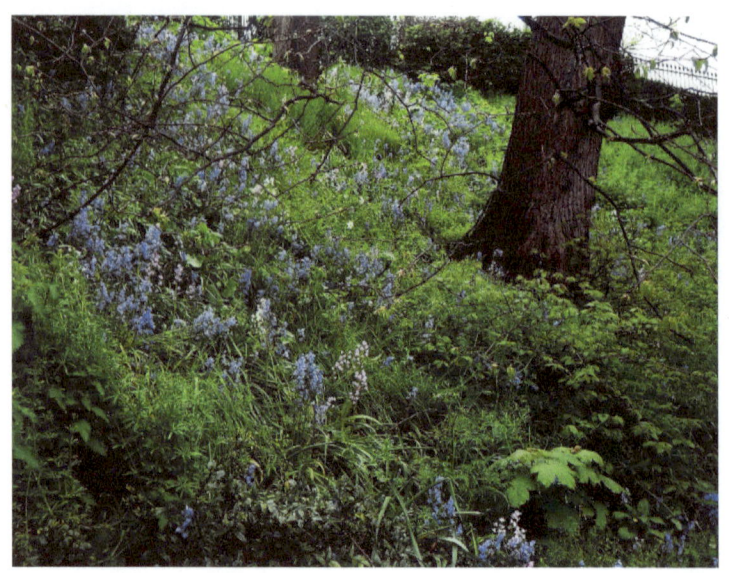

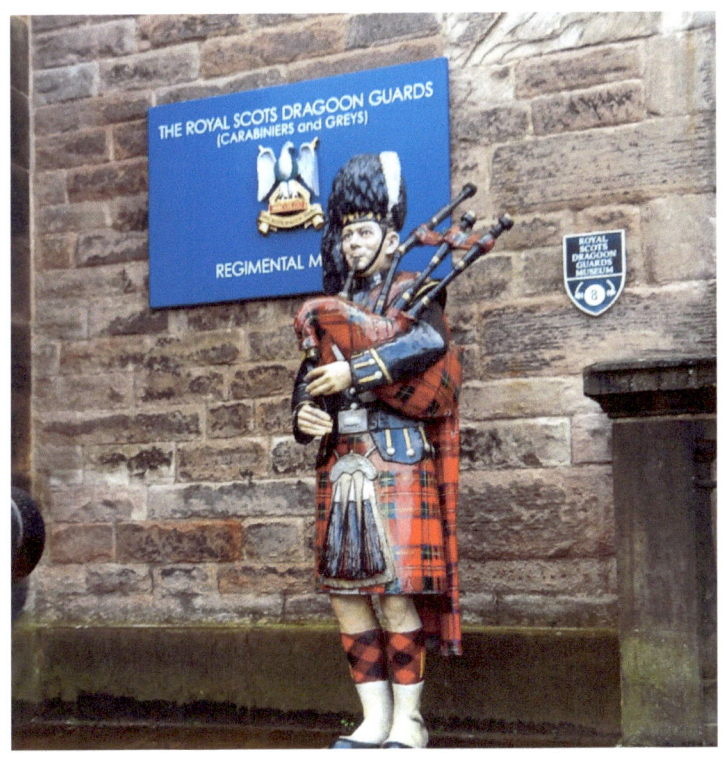

Inside Edinburgh castle,museums

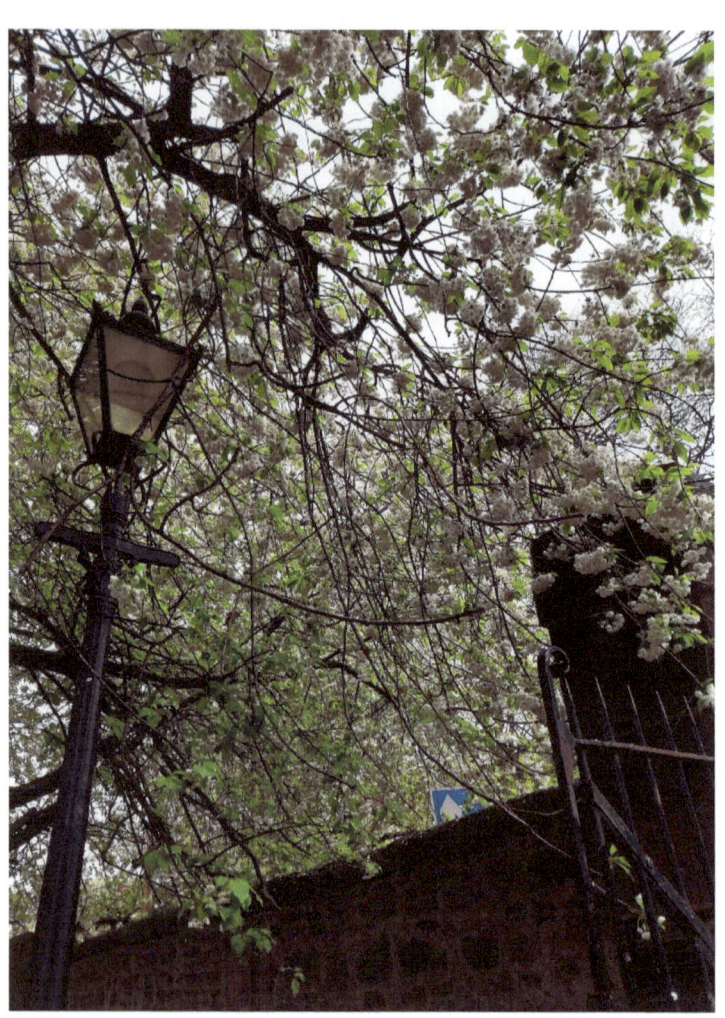

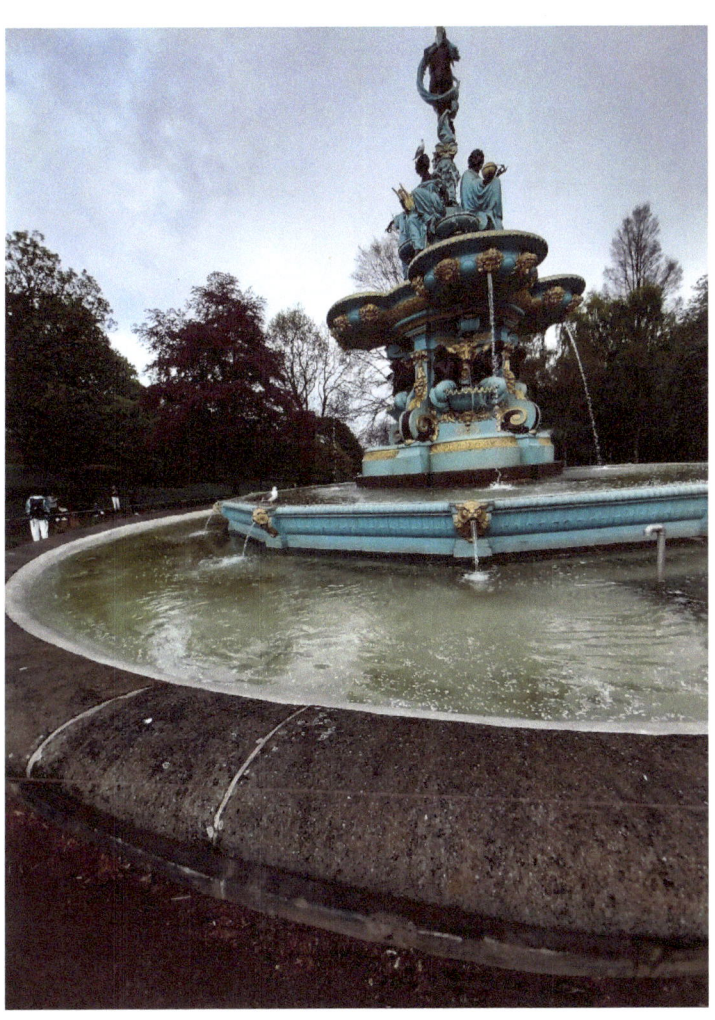

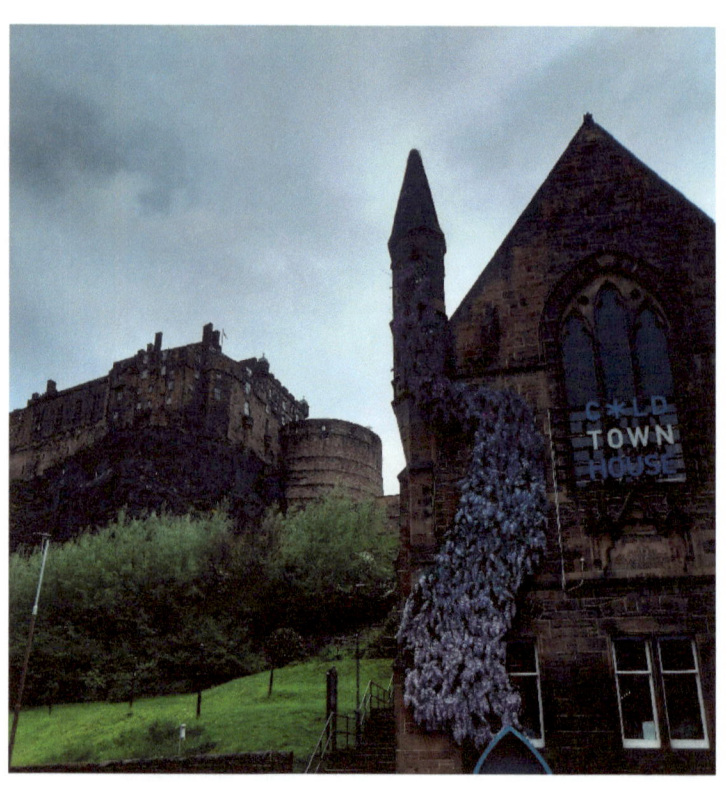

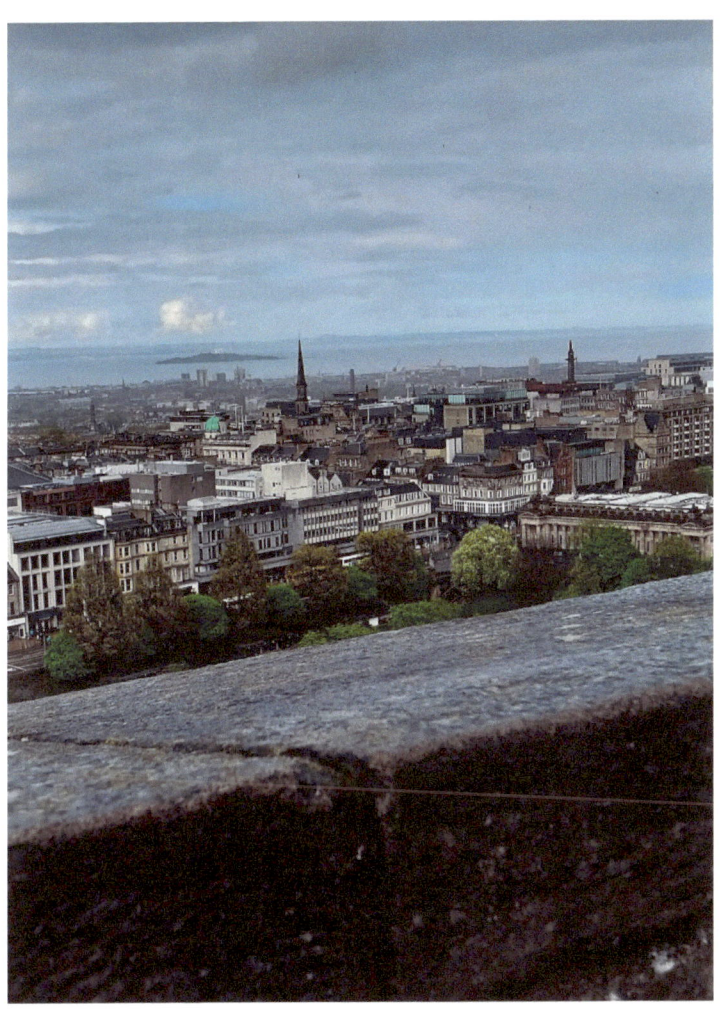

View from Edinburgh castle

At

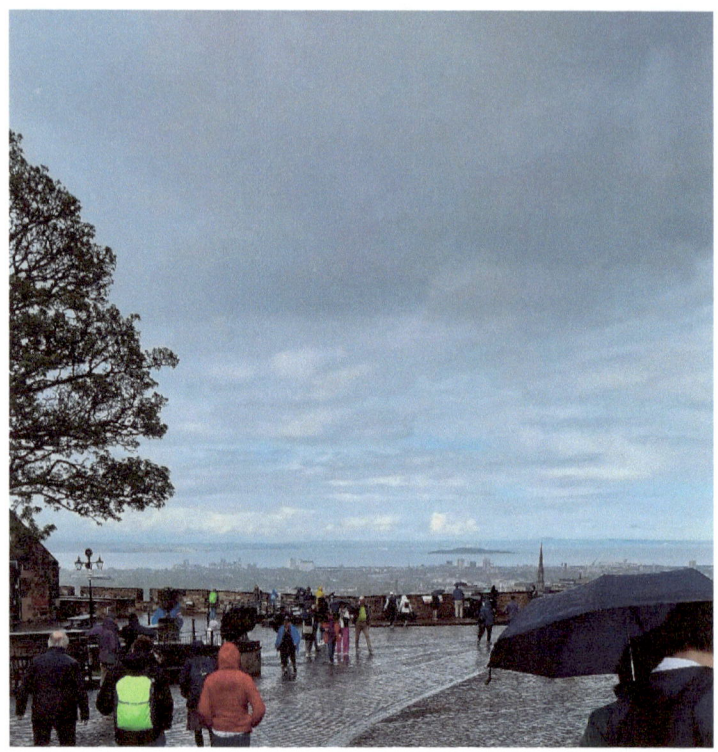

At Edinburgh castle

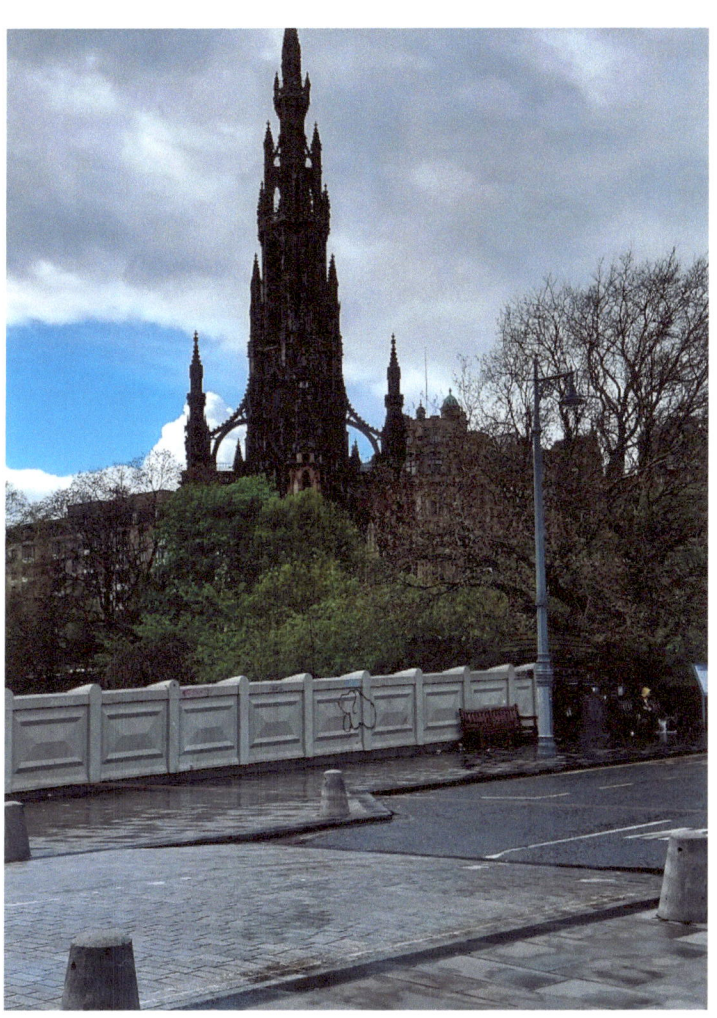

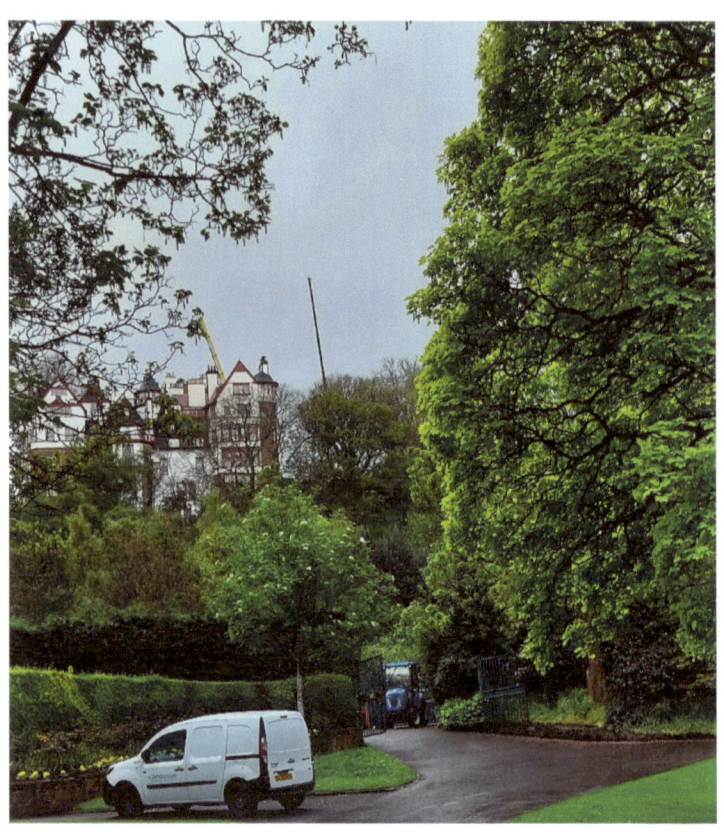

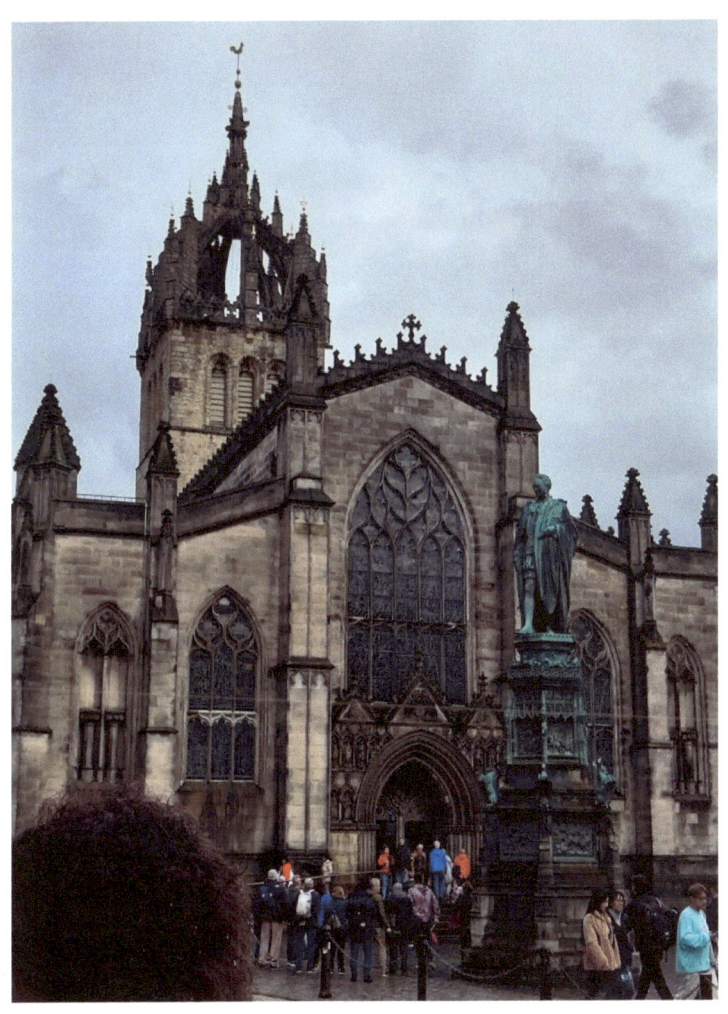

St Giles Cathedral

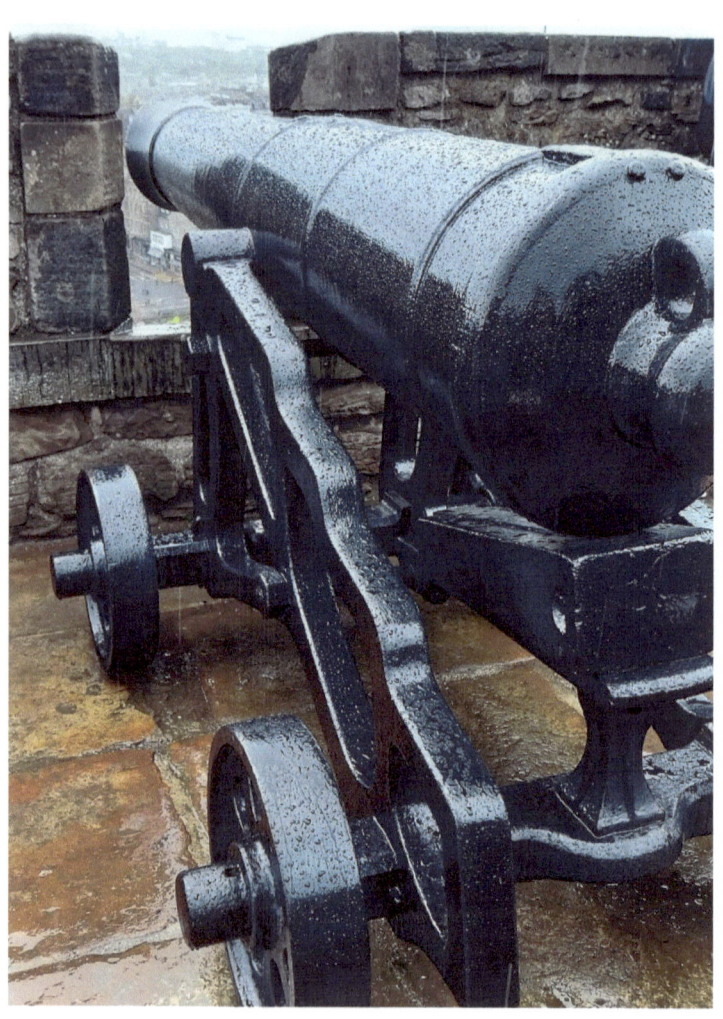

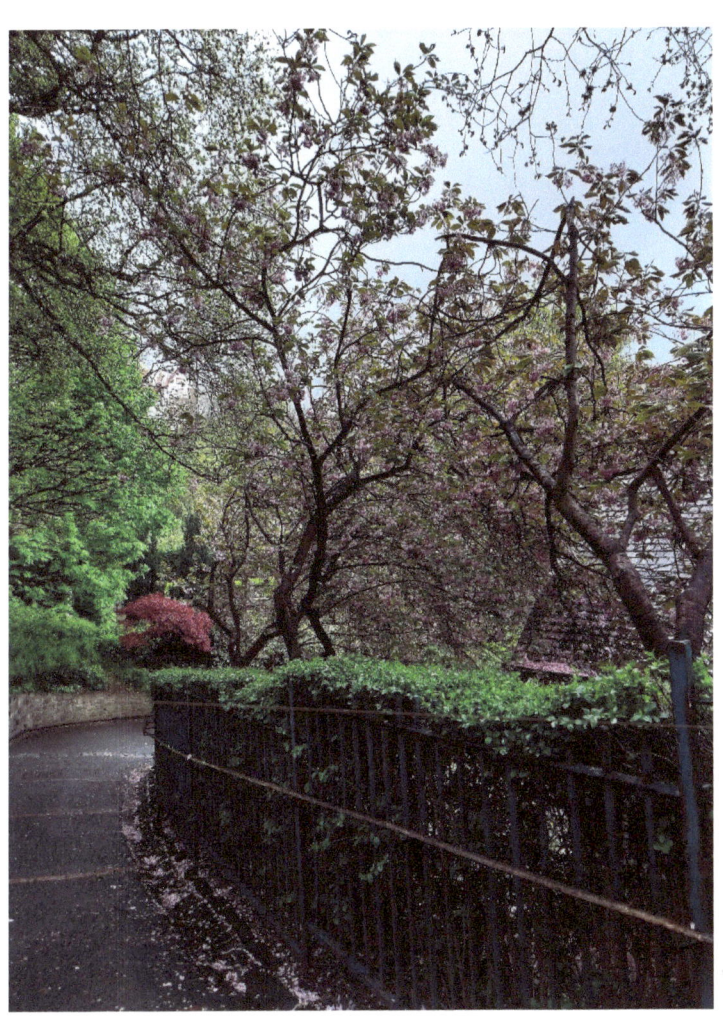

Glasgow

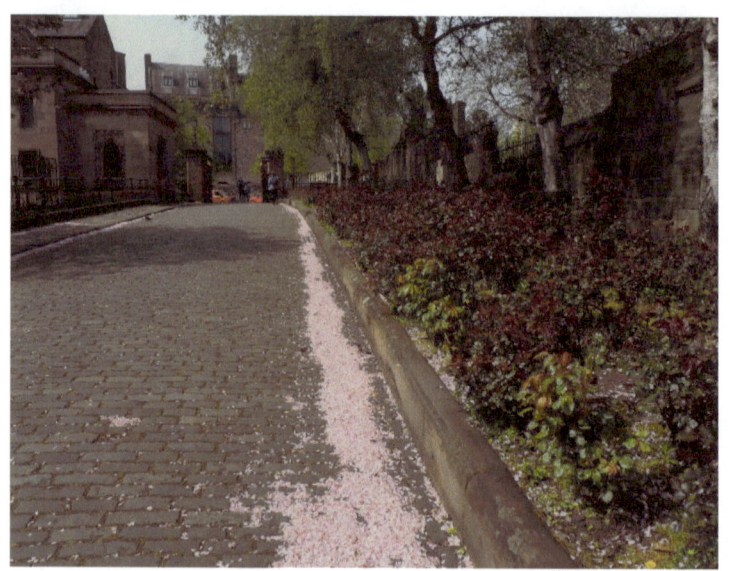

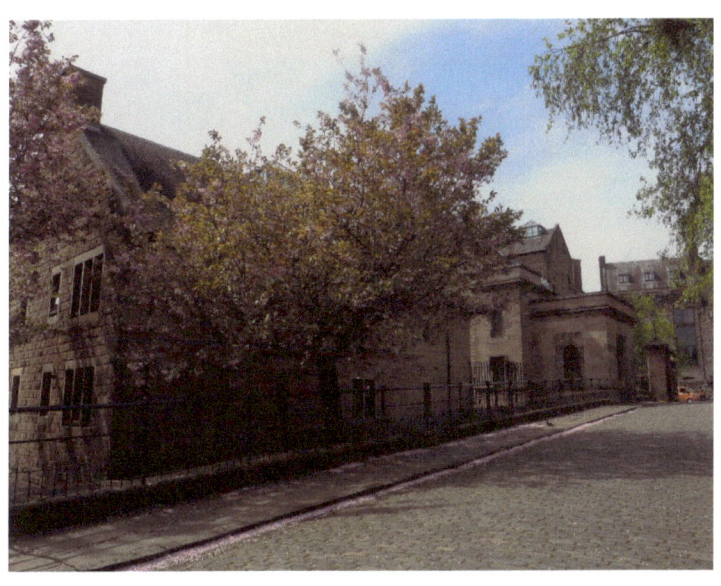

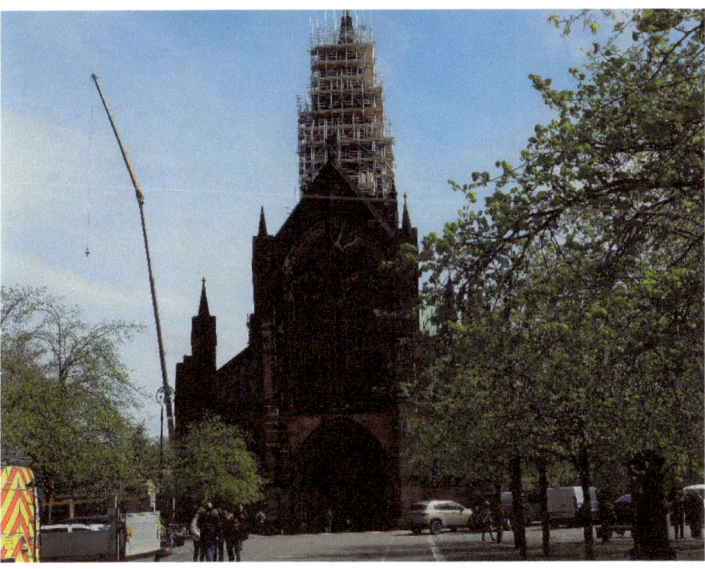

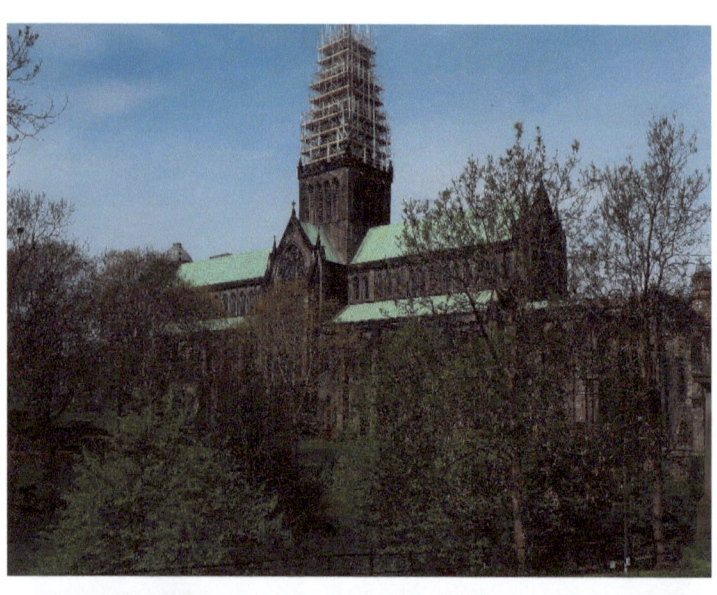

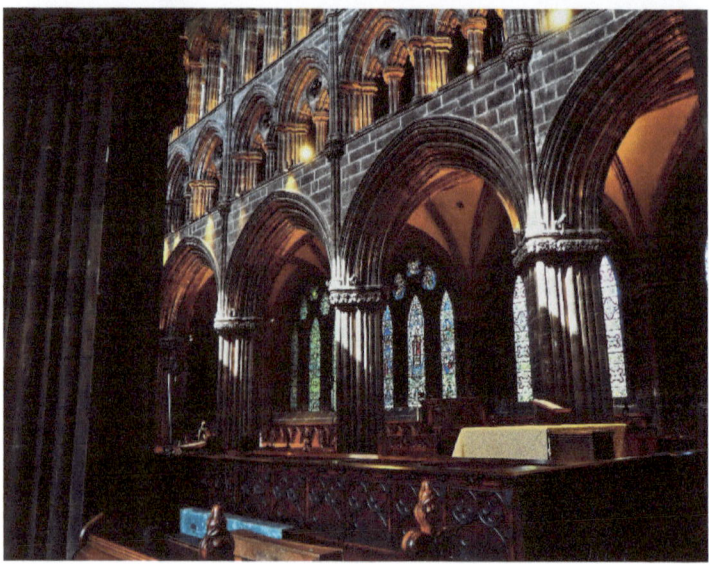

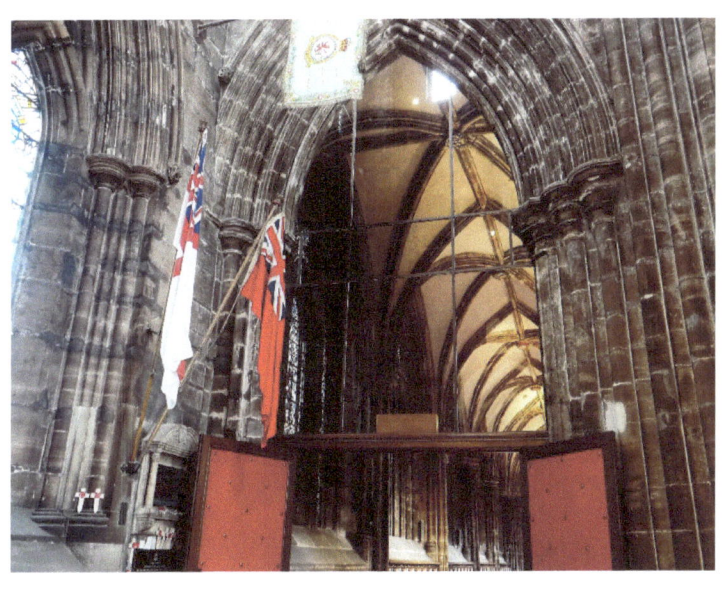

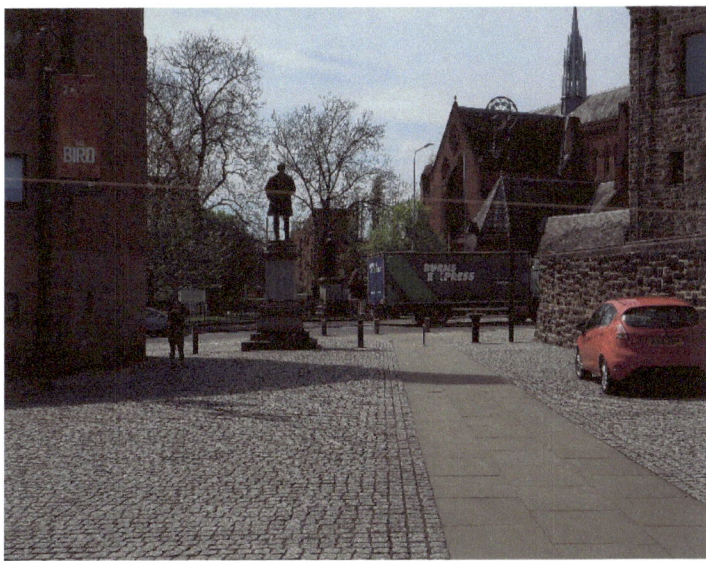

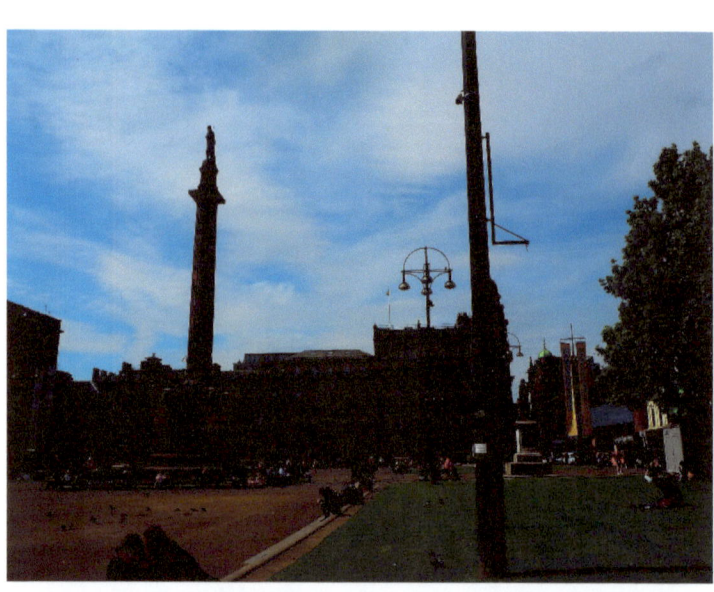

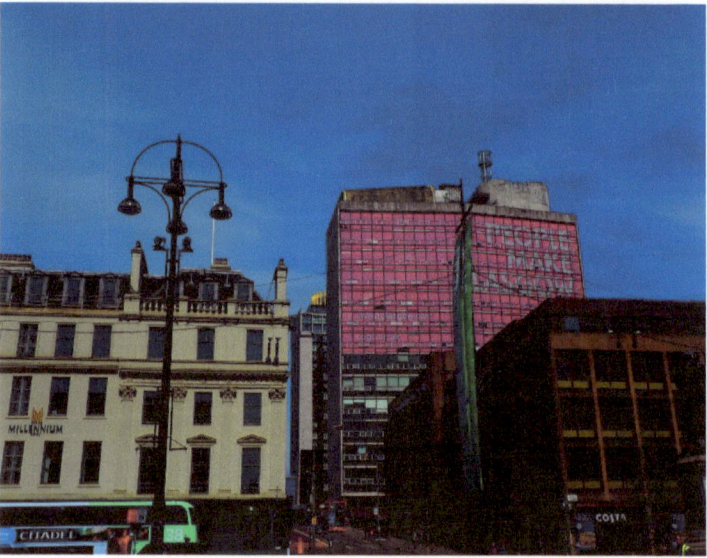

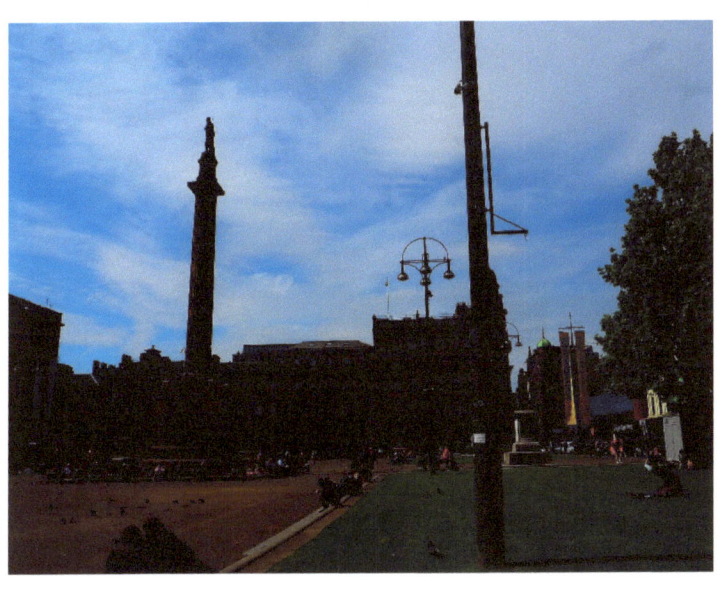

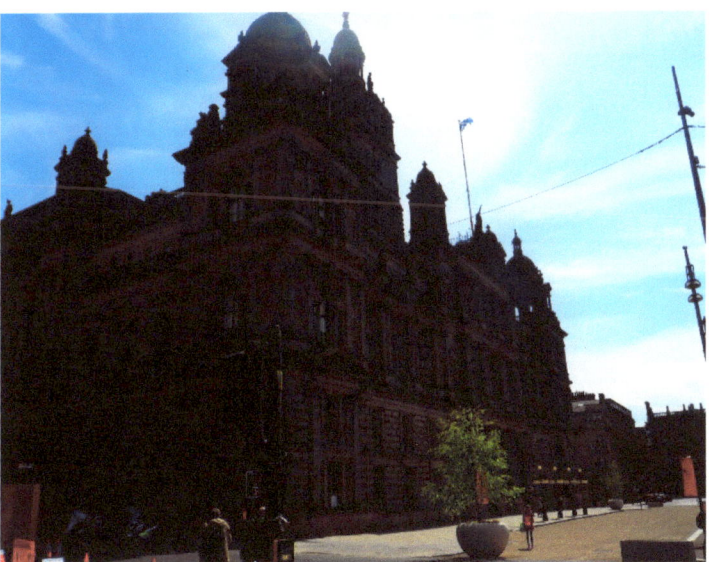

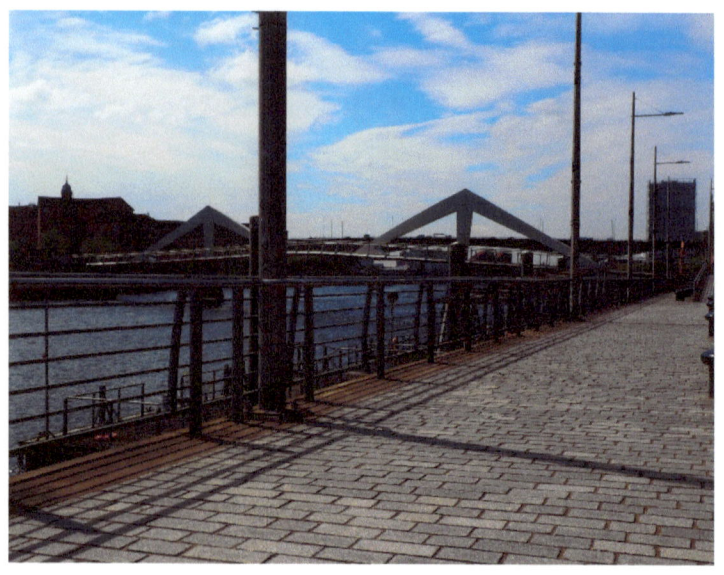

By the river..

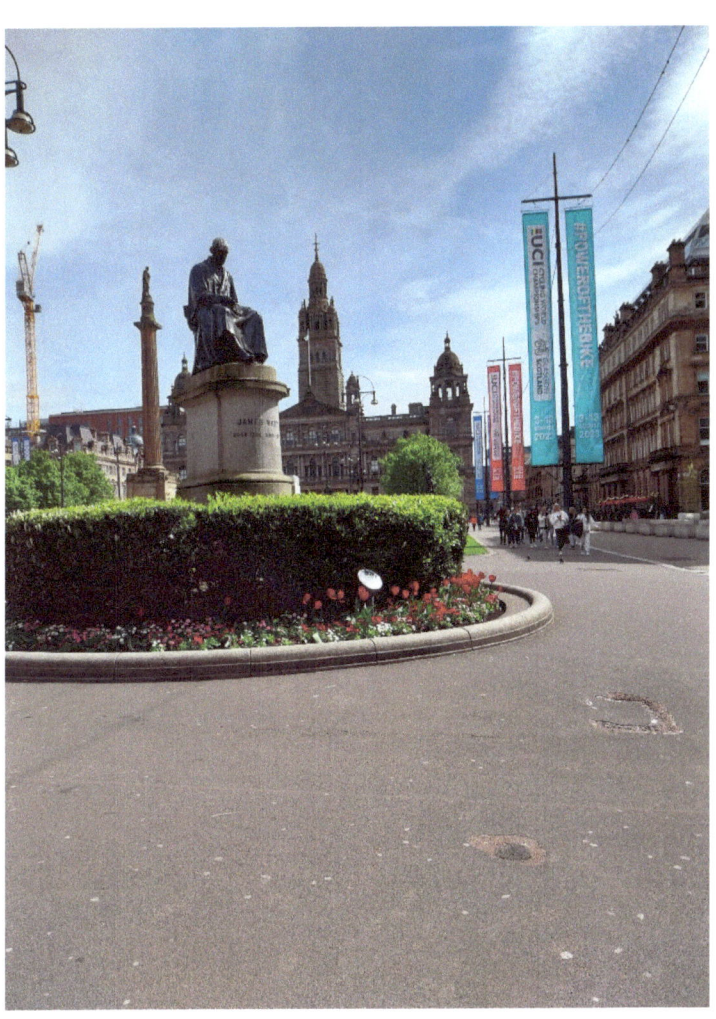

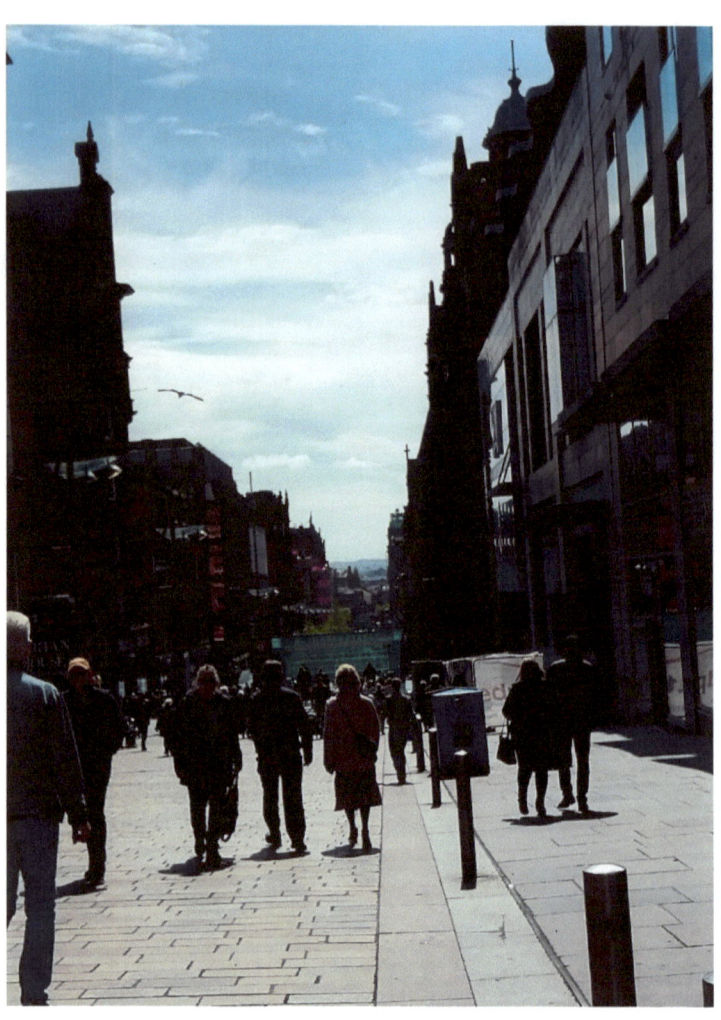

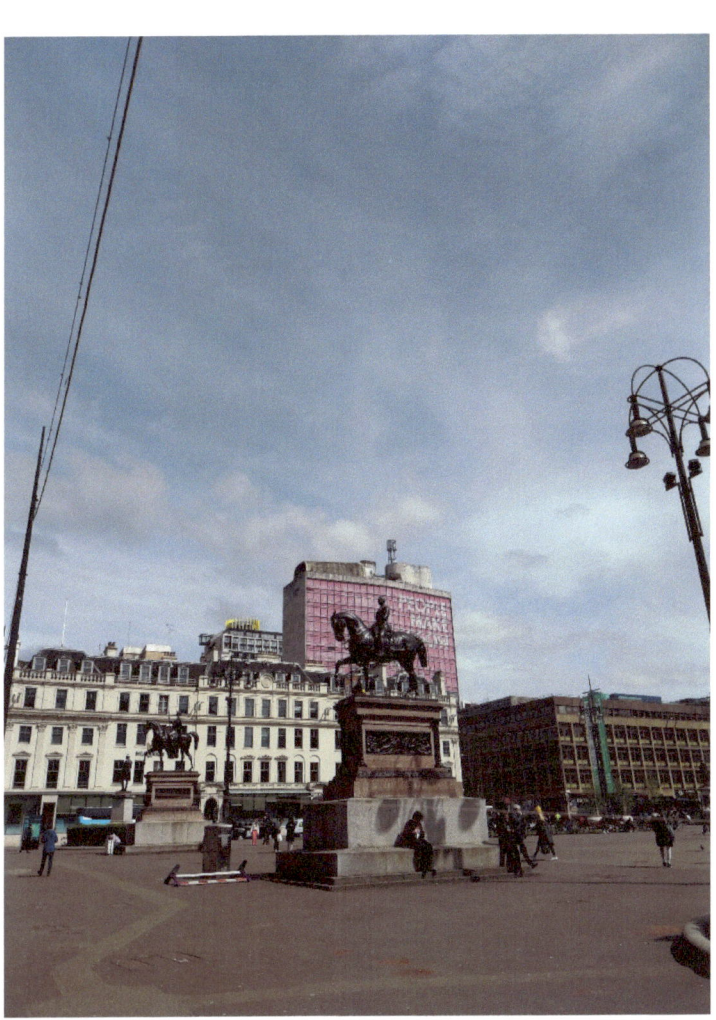

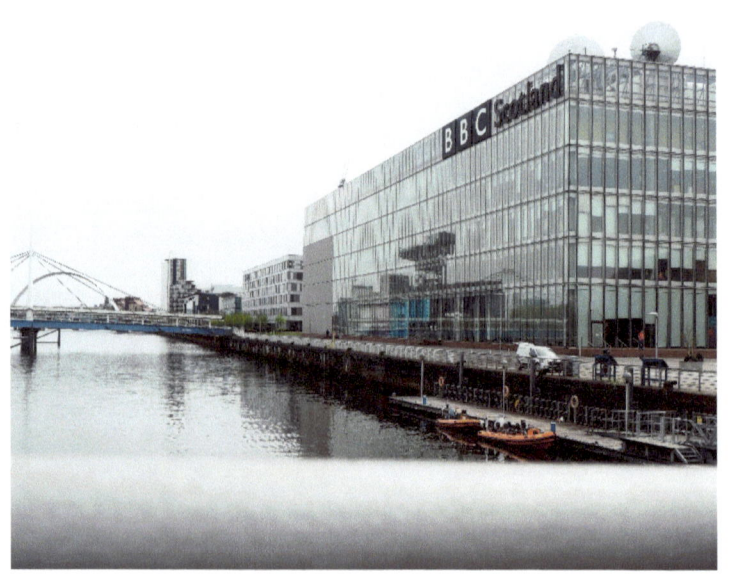

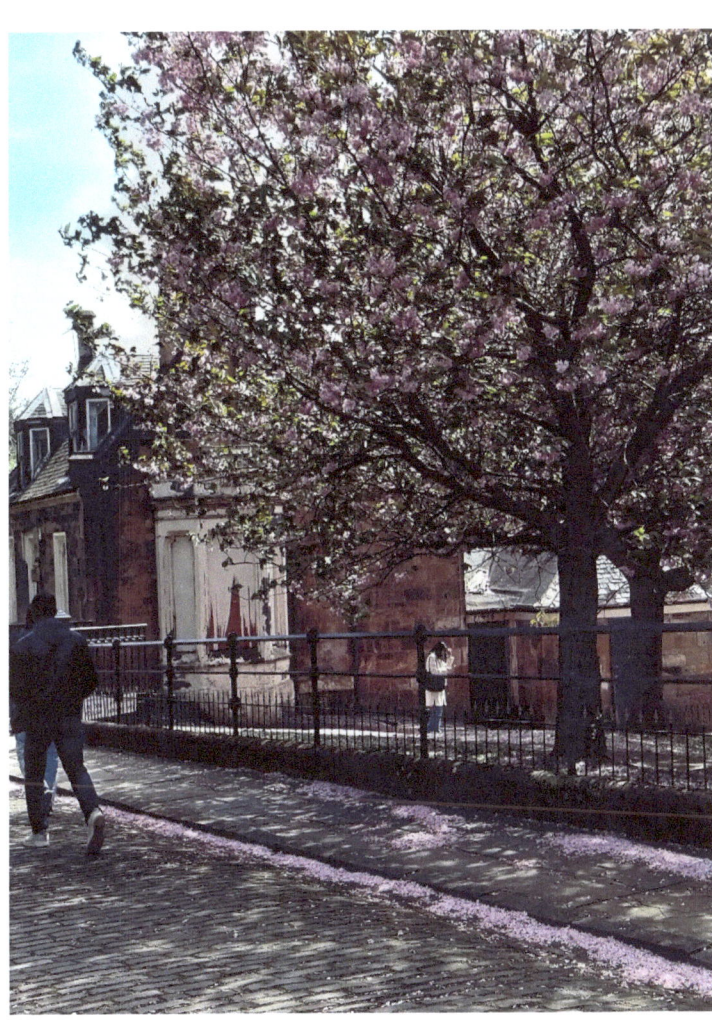

Well, as this is only photos-it cannot be any longer than this.

I hope someone enjoy the photos,if not I enjoy it myself. Especially days when I can't go anywhere.